For our dearly belated Lens & Melissa
with love a
for all th

Canyn.

HIRAETH

Deep Longing

Fifteen authors in search of their heartland

The ICE Pack

***

Book One

with gratitude to

The University of Cambridge: Institute of Continuing Education

First published in the United Kingdom in 2025 by WriteSpace Publishing
www.writespace.ink

Individual contributors are members of or guest writers for The ICE Pack
www.theicepack.org

Responsible for the content and design of this book:
Mana Jay, R. L. Shelley, Caryn Solomon & Fenna Williams
Cover Image: © R. Costa 2025
Editor: Mana Jay
Line and copy-editing: Margaret Kirk & Caryn Solomon

———————

ISBN Softcover: 978-1-917908-00-9
ISBN E-book: 978-1-917908-01-6

Contents

Special thanks

TO FENNA WILLIAMS

Driving force behind the creation of this book.

Winner of the Goldene Auguste 2024, coveted German crime literature award, Fenna is author, co-author, and editor of many widely appreciated books across different genres in Germany. She is now turning her hand to writing in English. This book would not have come to fruition without her.

FOREWORD

JESSICA J. LEE & DEREK NIEMANN

When fifteen people from five continents met for the first time in a virtual classroom during the loneliness of the pandemic, no one could have imagined they would go on to defeat another kind of isolation. The popular cliché is of the solitary writer toiling in a garret to produce their work. This book shatters that stereotype and gives us an uplifting new model.

The authors of this anthology all began this journey by signing up with us at Cambridge University for a creative writing course in a weekly meeting place online. The goal we set for them was to hone individual craft through mutual support. Read something new each week, converse with fellow students, and above all write something you hadn't imagined yourself trying before. Students learn from tutors, yes, but in this vulnerable yet exciting place of exchange, we learn from our students too.

Out of the many groups and students we had taught over the years, it became apparent that this group, this hitherto random collection of individuals, was exceptional. When they asked us to write this foreword, we felt it apt for them to sum up their experiences, too. One of our contributors noted, 'Learning something substantial about creative non-fictional writing I paid for, but learning about camaraderie rendered everything the more valuable.' Another observed that, 'There was kindness, support, and always encouragement.'

For us as tutors, what was striking was the sheer amount of shared motivation we found in the group — so much so that when this particular group's years of training and courses ran out, something remarkable happened. A magical combination of determination and the friendship that had developed drove these fifteen writers to stay together and seek a new objective, a new purpose. Hiraeth was born.

It has been a special kind of joy to witness this level of motivation and cooperative spirit amongst our writing students. So often, writers complete their courses and then venture into the world to write alone, much as we creative writing tutors do. But their learning journey was anything but over. The group plotted out a calendar full of meetings. They scheduled deadlines for sharing writing, planned group calls and workshopping. They opted to write in community — recognising how much stronger their words became through the act of sharing ideas, inspiration, criticism, and comfort. And while they could have left the course and us tutors behind, they offered us an invitation instead.

We followed on as we had left off from Cambridge — entirely fuelled by their desire to keep learning and growing. Each of us tutors took on former students to mentor in shaping their story. In group workshops we saw the writers grow in confidence as each offered constructive comments on the developing narratives. One of the group confided, 'My words feel heard, valued, and strengthened. Between us we exchange not just knowledge but the strength that comes from walking similar paths, facing similar challenges, and celebrating the same triumphs.'

Why Hiraeth? Perhaps, in part, the appeal of something that is both nebulous and specific. The word, lifted from the valleys of Wales, is capacious in meaning and yet also curiously indefinable. German 'Heimat' comes close, with every native speaker understanding a word that is resonant with notions of place, land and family. Somehow Hiraeth seemed to carry an extra quality that appealed to the group, a certain wistfulness that The University of Wales online dictionary tries to pin down, likening it to 'a homesickness tinged with grief and sadness over the lost or departed'. And yet perhaps it represents something more meaningful. Can it be a pure coincidence that so many members of this writing group are living beyond the country or even the continent of their birth? They met through the interstitial space of the internet, and through their collaboration have drawn lines of connection around the globe. They reflect the world we live in and the desire to find belonging, whether it is in a location or an emotion. Each of these diverse stories is searching for meaning, for understanding, for Hiraeth.

The authors may have written on their own, but they were never alone: on the group's lively chat, we watched from a distance as 'ideas bounced back and forth, suggestions sparked each other, creative confidence grew. Over the months in which this project developed, the common purpose bound us all, and boldness in trying out new ideas and approaches was fostered.' The openness, generosity, and kindness with which they handled one another's tender ideas and vulnerability was a marvel to behold. As they told us, 'No idea is too fanciful and if your flights of fantasy run awry the landing is always soft.'

A common thread in this truly collaborative venture was the realisation among the writers that it was possible to take risks. 'Writing is such a personal act,' said one, 'and sharing unfinished work with others can be intimidating. But when you're surrounded by people who genuinely care about your success and are willing to be vulnerable themselves, it builds a profound sense of safety.' So developed an ethos that might have been forbidding in another environment — even in the classroom format from which the group had emerged — experiment and submit. But here, each writer held the others. They learned to stand alone, and together.

This has been an eye-opening experience for us tutors in how far cooperative writing can go. And a lesson in the vital need for community as part of the writing process. Now the work is submitted to a wider audience and you, dear reader, are invited to meet the group. We hope you will enjoy this beautiful collection.

Dr Jessica J. Lee and Derek Niemann,
   Tutors of creative writing at the University of Cambridge, December 2024

Kalahari Klip

Caryn Solomon

KGALAGADI (KALAHARI)

Thousands of miles of waterless, ancient desert where sand is red, termites build houses with spires pointing north and rain is alive with a scent that hits you before you see it. Where parched, stunted camel-thorn trees the colour of dust are fiercely adorned with bleached-white, needle-sharp thorns so long you can use them to tie up your hair, and shimmering, scorched-bark air pretends to be water. Deserts can be deceiving.

The place where the oldest human DNA[1] lives — a few thousand Khoisan people who still hunt and gather for survival, who know that we humans are no more than small creatures in one, infinite land-scape, no more than dots, motes in a cosmos where 'I' is no different from stardust.

---

1. The Bushmen (San people) were the first human inhabitants of Southern Africa; there is evidence that they have been living there continuously as nomadic hunter-gatherers for over twenty thousand years. https://www.independent.co.uk/news/science/world-s-most-ancient-race-traced-in-dna-study-1677113.html

The place where dry, yellow grass tangled itself around my heart,
where I fell in love before I could talk.

Upington, Northern Cape, South Africa (1953-1957)

Sand

Take off our dresses.
Fall down.
Roll in the sand in our *broekies*, our panties.
Stand up and stir with our toes.
Fall down and roll again.
Sit up and rock, backwards and forwards.
Lena shouts, '*Kom! Laat ons lag*!'/Come! Let's laugh!
Laugh and laugh until we cry.

That is the game we play every day, while Mommy looks after the baby and Daddy is fixing sick people.

Our front yard is a field of red earth. Soft, red sand with clumps of yellow grass in between. You have to be careful rolling around — that grass is dry and spiky.

I am four. Lena is twelve. She lives with us. Her brothers and sisters and granny live in a small house in the *lokasie*, the location.[2] Her knees are the colour of biscuits, like the *bokkies,* the baby impala that sometimes walk into our yard to eat our tomatoes. I like her hair, curly like mine, but shorter and fluffy, and the sound of her laugh, like crickets at night. Most of all, I like her stories and songs.

Lena says the sky is a blue balloon, with us and the sun inside it. She says if I look at the sun my eyes will burn, and I won't be able to

---

2. Informal segregated township where 'non-white' people lived during Apartheid.

see anymore. Once, when she wasn't looking at me, I looked. The brightness hurt and my eyes squeezed shut on their own. Daddy told me the sun is a ball of fire, with flames so hot you can fry an egg on the front of the car at midday.

By the time the sun reaches the middle of the sky, Lena and I are covered in red. The air feels like I'm standing in front of the oven when Mommy takes out biscuits we made. It makes the back of my neck all sticky. Wiping my face with my hands makes something go up my nose. It feels like *songololos,* millipedes, crawling in there, but it's not them — it's tiny pieces of sand, dry like ash, dry like the sound of *sonbesies,* cicadas.

The roof of our house is greyish green, like the skin of a fig. When pods drop from the blue-gum trees that stand at the back of the house, I can hear them ping. Daddy says they make that sound because the roof is made of tin. On the edge of the roof, brown patches that Lena calls rust, which comes from rain. I've never seen that. She says that water comes down from the sky once in a blue moon. I don't think she means it — the moon is usually yellow or white, sometimes orange or brownish red, but I've never seen one that's blue. Anyway, how can water fall out of the sky?

When it's too hot outside, we play on the *stoep,* the wide verandah that goes all the way round our house. Mommy brings out a tray with a jug of Ribena juice, blocks of ice, two mugs, and a plate of Marie biscuits. Across the top of the jug is a white doily covered in beads — red, green, and yellow. Lena made it to stop the bees and the flies from drowning.

We fill up our inside-cheeks and sloosh the sweet, purple coldness around our mouths for as long as we can before we swallow. The biscuits are stuck together with butter. We slide them apart and lick off the butter, slowly with big licks, until they are soggy and falling apart.

The big, soft-cushion chair in the corner of the stoep is where I pile my dolls. They are all naked. Some don't have arms and legs. When it's their bedtime, Lena and I choose who will be our baby. Sometimes we choose two each. Then we put them into the bed that Daddy made from a box that used to hold lemons. The smell stayed, even after Lena and I painted it white. Then we lie down on the cool, hard floor on our backs, with our legs and arms out wide. The smell of wax polish makes me feel sleepy. I slide against Lena and put my head in her lap. Then she sings:

'*Lam-tietie, dam-tietie[3] doo-doo my liefietjie[4]*
Lam-tieite, dam-tietie doo-doo my blommetjie[5]
Lam-tietie, dam-tietie doo-doo-doooo
Lam-tietie, dam-tieitie doo-doo-doooo'

Over and over, 'til we all fall asleep.

Some afternoons, the sky goes dark and faraway curtains hang down. They look like smoke. Daddy says it's water from clouds called cumulonimbus, and the flashes of white light in the sky are fire, but not the same as the sun.

Then comes the growling, like Flinky our dog when someone touches his food while he's eating. Lena says it's an angry bull in the sky — we have to pray, to make him go, to call the cow to bring us her milk.

When the growling gets louder, Daddy and Mommy stand on the stoep shading their brows, watching the sand and the grass blowing across the yard. When they look up at the sky, their faces go yellowish green.

'Maybe today...'

'I wish...'

'...how much longer...'

I don't understand what they're talking about, but I know it's something about the bull and the cow and big people are sad.

---

3. Afrikaans pet names for a baby, untranslatable
4. Sleep little love
5. Sleep little flower

Rain

I smell it long before it arrives. That's what happens — the scent always comes first. But I don't know that then, have no recollection to draw on or language to name it.

I've never smelled anything like this before. I lift my nose, like Flinky does when he's sniffing the dustbin, and take big breaths — it feels like my nostrils are drinking.

The sky is the colour of wood after a fire — flashes of silver are cracking it open — the bull is growling again — hot wind scratching my eyes with dust from the ground is making me cry. Something drops on my foot — warm like a stone, but soft. I wiggle my toes and shake my leg. It's wet! Then more heavy wetness — onto my hair and my hands. Then more and more — coming down faster and faster — and growling and growling, louder and louder — arms and shoulders covered in water — the sand is turning to mud like when we spray with the hosepipe, but there's no hosepipe, just water spilling and crashing down from the sky — someone is throwing it out of a bucket, but there's no bucket, just water and fire exploding all over the sky, booming and growling, hurting my ears.

'Lena, where are you? Lena, Lena! *Kom, Lena!*'/Come, Lena!

I need you to hold my hand — because I am crying, because I am scared, because of the angry bull up there, or maybe a giant, making a horrible banging and smashing, bashing inside my head, the purple sky is making me shiver, the fire that's not the sun is breaking the sky, the giant bull roaring and roaring, please make him stop! Flinky is howling, but Lena is laughing and dancing and jumping all over the yard, not looking at me, and now I'm all covered in mud, because I fell down, running to catch her. LENA! Stop waving your arms, I want my mommy!

I'm screaming, but no one can hear me, my throat is choking, the giant is coming down here to eat us up when he's finished weeing on us.

And then I'm in Lena's arms in the chair on the stoep.

5

'*O my wêreld! Dis ou vrouens met knobkieries reen!*'/Oh, my world! It's raining old women with clubs!

She tells me it's called a thunder and lightning storm — the bull has lost his way and now he's charging all over the sky, growling and shooting light from his eyes to help him see where to go. But he doesn't eat children.

Then she sings, '*Lamtietie, damtietie, doo-doo my liefstetjie.*'

Some men have arrived with wooden boxes called tea chests. Mommy says it's time to pack up. Plates, pots, pans, glasses, cups, knives, forks, sheets, towels, beds, chairs, tables, books, pictures, our clothes, all Daddy's papers and instruments from his surgery, and all the rest of the furniture. Even Mommy's sewing machine, my dolls, and their bed. All into the tea chests.

Mommy says we're sailing to England. We'll be on a ship, the *Athlone Castle*, for two weeks, on a big water called sea. I'll be able to see my dolls again when we unpack the boxes, in our new home, while Daddy does his FRCS[6], which will teach him more things about how to fix people's legs. But I don't like those men, taking our things, throwing them into old boxes meant for tea.

'*Lena, Lena, waar is jy?*'/ Lena, Lena, where are you?

She's on the stoep, bending over her white bucket making a washing sound, squelching her hands together without looking up, but she knows I'm there. Then she stops, pats her hands on her dress, and we run down the front steps into the red yard. She's still not looking at me.

We don't feel like playing *Kom laat ons lag*. So we sit on the ground, next to each other, and cross our legs. Nobody speaks.

After a long time, Lena starts swishing her hands across the red sand. Back. Forward. Back. Forward. Over and over. All of a

---

6. Fellowship of the Royal College of Surgeons (FRCS) — professional qualification required to practise as a surgeon in the United Kingdom.

sudden, she stretches backwards, closes her fingers, puts her hand in my lap and laughs — the sound of crickets at night.

Her fingers open. A pip rolls out. It looks like one from a sweet, Kakamas[7] peach. Dark orange with folds and wrinkles. I take the pip from my lap, but no, it's not that — it's a small stone from our yard.

'Dis jou Kalahari klip liefie. Hou dit styf — altyd.'/It's your Kalahari stone, sweetheart. Hold it tight — always.

She slides her arm like a snake over my shoulder.

I close my hand round the stone and think about where to hide it — far away from the box-men.

A long lorry has taken the boxes away.

Our house is empty.

Mommy, Daddy, Baby and I walk down the steps from the stoep, across the red sand to the iron gate.

Lena walks behind us. Shluff, shluff, shluff, shluff — I can hear her bare feet slapping the warm sand. Then the sound stops. I turn around. She's standing still. Her face looks like the wooden mask that hung on the wall behind Daddy's desk. My hand slides into my pocket, my hiding place.

'Kom, Lena! LENA! KOM!'/Come, Lena! LENA! COME!

'Ag leifie, ek kom nie...'/Aah sweetheart, I'm not coming.

I try to speak, but a great balloon is blowing up in my chest, closing my throat — I can't breathe, my whole body is shaking, the skin's falling off, melting like wax down a candle, I want to smack Lena's face to make her start walking again, but she can't, because all around her the red earth is rising — a huge red wave — knocking her down, crashing straight through her, into my ears, my eyes, up my nose — I can't see her — everything's numb.

Except my fingers — holding tight — my Kalahari *klip*.

---

7. Northern Cape

CROSSING

Athlone Castle, Atlantic Ocean (December 1957)

Surrounded by water and sky, for days and nights on end, you could barely tell one from the other.

At night, beyond the ship, a single blackness, festooned with sparkles. Above us, glittering constellations whose stories I knew — giants' belts, horses with men's heads, the Milky Way, the Southern Cross, which my father had taught me to use as a magic way to find South. Alongside the ship, living bodies of light — fish, squid, tiny crustaceans, algae — and moonlight tripping in watery peaks and streams, reflections of stars. Days, a translucent bleeding and blooming of white, yellow, silver, and pinks, and blues, and greens. I'd never seen such things before.

The constant dip and tilt of the ship and my father pointing out new constellations as we moved north were all that kept me alive to the fact of our moving — without perspective and landmarks, and not conceiving north and south in any material way, the moving was little more than a random rocking — it certainly wasn't a moving 'to' or 'from'.

I didn't see the Southern Cross disappear — one night it just wasn't there. I wouldn't have understood then that it wasn't the stars slipping away — nor that this was the start of a lifetime encountering myself as constantly moving, myriad selves incorporating every place that I'd live in and leave behind, remaining the outsider, longing to move 'back', learning along the way, like Lot's wife, that it's best not to look over your shoulder.

THE TIME BETWEEN

Wimbledon, London, England (1958-1961)

It's forty-five steps from the street up to our Wimbledon flat. I count them every time. My job is unlocking the front door, because Mom is carrying my little brother and bags full of food.

Inside, it's dark and cold and smells of gas — a new smell to me. To turn on the heater, Mom puts money into a box on the wall.

Then I help to unpack the shopping. But first I must take off my new Wellington boots ('Be careful, no mud on the floor!'). I pull as hard as I can, to make them let go of my feet. Lena and I never had boots, we didn't even have shoes — just bare feet, on the sand, which was sometimes too hot to stand on. The stoep was cool, but we had to hold our toes tightly together, or else we might slip.

I like my new, navy-blue coat, especially the wooden buttons that look like peanuts. Not the peanuts they give you to feed the Trafalgar Square pigeons, the ones with hard shells that Lena and I cracked open with stones. I don't like my gloves. My fingers stay frozen, and I can't feel the edges of anything.

The day we arrived at our new home it was snowing. Specks of white floating down from the sky, piling like anthills, but softer and wet. When I touched them, my fingers burned. I didn't know cold could do that. Mom called them snowflakes. They looked like ice cream. I let a few land on my tongue — they melted and tasted of nothing. We jumped in the piles and scooped up as much as our hands could hold, to make balls to throw at each other. I liked the throwing, but not getting hit. Snowflake balls are almost as hard as hail.

Since then, it has snowed twice and rained every day. But not big drops like the rain that comes from a bull or a cow. Raindrops here are small and sneaky — you have to look hard and put out your hand to see if they really are there. Usually they are, all day, making a few drippy sounds, pretending they're almost finished, or on their way somewhere else, but they aren't — they stay and stay and then stop, but not always. Sometimes a few drops keep falling, like when you don't turn the tap off enough.

At lunchtime, Mom makes strips of bread called soldiers, and soft-boiled eggs. My chair is next to the window. It's hard to see out through the wet, runny-nose glass. I can't see sun or sky outside — just greyish brown, like bath water after we've washed off the mud. Then it gets dark, long before bedtime. While I'm waiting for supper, I sit on the floor in front of the fire (Fire! INSIDE!) and make up stories using my new words — mist, fog, sleet, snow, damp, frost, duffle-coat, mittens, drizzle, puddle, and snowdrops — beautiful, white flowers, hanging like tiny bells.

When I climb into bed, the sheets are wet, always wet. Mom gives me a cuddle. 'They're not really wet, just a bit cold. You'll soon warm up,' she says. But I can feel wet. Wet every night. On the ceiling, grey splotches, like bruises. Then Mom says 'damp'. Before she closes the curtains, I look out the window. I never see stars.

One thing I love is the smell of my wet scarf. It reminds me of being in the yard giving Flinky a bath with the hosepipe — splashing his face, making him bark, lying with him to dry off on the sunny part of the stoep, hearing his pink tongue flap, feeling his breath on my cheek, smelling his tummy.

I also love school and Bella, my teacher. She loves laughing, like me and Lena. But Bella is soft and round. Lena's elbows are sharp. Bella's surname is Zusman. Sounding it out with a loud 'ZUS!' makes me want to jump up and open my arms out wide. Which we do when we play the reading game:

Lay the flash cards out on the floor,
In a long line,
With spaces between them.
Jump over them one at a time.
With each jump, throw up your arms.
Shout out the word you see on the card.

Bella says I know all the words because I could read before

coming to school. She gives me books to take home. When I bring them back the next day, she makes her eyes big and says, 'Eating up words for supper again — no baked beans on toast?' When I tell her I don't like baked beans she laughs and gives me a hug.

My favourite subject is singing. My favourite song is 'All Things Bright and Beautiful'. When we sing it, I close my eyes and see sand — red sand — Lena, laughing and singing — clumps of grass — yellow grass — and hear the bull, growling.

When Spring arrived, we played in the park. There, green was a verb — vibrating, alive, pregnant with water — I'd seen it before, in books — no green could have been less like the dusty membrane of khaki, the fig-skin green of our tin roof that coated everything trying to grow in waterless earth beneath a cloudless sky without end. In England the sky fell inwards — a soggy, grey sponge, sucking up clouds, the stars, itself. There was little that happened to make me look up. Longing for what I couldn't name, I made up stories, and read, and read.

My diet of English children's literature took me into a history of kings and queens and knights of round tables. Brave, honourable, strong in their service to others, they went into battle sheathed in metal — no inch of skin exposed. Bearing long swords, lances of wood with iron tips, steel-headed maces, axes, and daggers, they'd boldly go on their horses to weather the storm.

*But that wasn't for me! For me, being brave was running into the heart of the storm **without** your clothes, not armoured from head to toe. I wanted to strip to my bare bones, to fling myself into the light-ning, hail, 'all-shaking thunder*[8] *and pounding rain of a deafening African storm, stark naked, arms spread-eagled, face to the sky, mouth wide, ready to swallow, eyes streaming, squelching the warm mud with my toes, wrapped in the smell of stone — dry earth yearning for water. I wanted to BE the storm.*

---

8. William Shakespeare, *King Lear*: Act 3, Scene 2.

Belmont, Boston, USA (1961-1962)

My father couldn't refuse an invite to join the team of Professor Otto Aufranc, world-renowned pioneer in the surgical replacement of damaged hips. It would be eighteen months at Massachusetts General — teaching hospital for Harvard Medical School.

Boston isn't our real home, but I love our big house, all made of wood called clapboard. In winter we have a big fire, with logs from the woods that smell delicious, not like the coal fire in England, which makes me cough. Here we toast marshmallows, pink and white. I like the white ones. The toasted, melty bits taste like toffee.

Beneath the house, there's a space for snow to pile up in winter — just big enough for me to squeeze into. To be by myself. Away from the kids who say I have to say 'kids' because 'children' means babies. Kids who stick out their tongues, say 'ugh' and make ugly faces, as if they feel sick, when I tell them that jelly is something we make at home with powder and boiling water, then eat it out of a bowl, when it's cold, with a spoon. At school, they stand in a circle around me at playtime — they call it 'recess' — and tell me I'm dumb because I don't know what 'jeans-and-sneakers' means, and laugh at my grey, pleated skirt, long, white socks, and brown, lace-up shoes, and the way I speak.

'Say something! Say something.'

'What do you want me to say?'

And then they shout 'What-t-t! What-t-t!', laughing at me because I said 't' at the end of 'what' before I said 'do'. *They* say 'Whadayou' — no 't', just the 'd'. I try to say it, but can't, then they shout 'Kwiddit' — a name they call me a lot. Why do they call me that? They know my real name is Caryn.

Under the house I forget all of that. I'm here with my favourite things: *Little House in the Big Woods*, by Laura Ingalls Wilder — I've read it so many times, I can open it up at any page and go on reading from there — and my Kalahari *klip*, in the silky bag that Mom made from her leftover sewing. When I'm tired of reading, I hold it and talk to Lena. I know she can hear me.

How did I know?

The rush of blood in my head and infusion of warmth through my body, whenever I thought of Lena, was message enough that the 'left behind' wasn't entirely something 'out there'. It was also something under my skin. Something inside. Traces within. My klip was not a dead object — it carried our voices, our ears, our games and our stories, Lena's and mine. Closing my fingers around it, I knew that stories go on and on, that we were still playing 'Kom laat ons lag'.

Mill Hill, London, UK (1962-1964)

My new school is ugly — a red-brick, two-storey rectangle with white-painted, steel windows. But two things I like are the garden — the willow tree and the small pond — and Outings, especially to old places like the Tower of London, to see the two little princes' blood on the walls of the dungeon.

Here, there aren't any teachers like Bella. These ones tell me I talk too much, and I shouldn't be reading books meant for adults. Like *Great Expectations*.

My friend is Jacqueline Lewis. Not the one in my class, with shiny-blue bows at the end of her plaits, who never asks me to play with her. The *other* Jacqueline Lewis, my friend, has the same hair, but she doesn't mind me calling them braids like the kids did in Boston — and she always asks me to play.

For the two years I went to that school, my mother believed she was real. Or so I thought.

Johannesburg, South Africa (1964-1976)

Another sailing. My father has taken the Chair of Orthopaedic Surgery at Witwatersrand University.

Here, at Parktown Girls' High, I'm eleven, two years younger than everyone in my class. They weren't four when they started school.

Everyone here knows how to swim. I can't even tread water. No one I knew in London could. Miss Rothgeiser tramps on my hands when I grab the side of the pool — she doesn't care if I sink. I've written a 'Caryn can't swim today, she's having her period' letter on Dad's prescription note paper. It was easy to trace his signature off an old cheque I found on his desk. Swimming lessons are twice a week. Changing into our costumes makes me feel scared and angry all at the same time. I hate that I'm the only one not wearing a bra. I can only use the letter one week a month, but it's better than nothing. I haven't even started my periods yet.

I'm good at running. Rothgieser knows that — I showed her my medal from Mill Hill — but she says I can't play team netball or tennis or hockey because I wear glasses. Anyway, Mom won't let me play hockey in case my ankles get smashed. That's because she was a ballet dancer. I'm not — I'm pigeon-toed and my arms are too long for my body. At matches, my job is to carry the half-time, iced, quartered oranges onto the field and hand them out to the thirsty players. The rest of the time, I sit on the side, watching.

School work is boring — we spend whole lessons copying down what the teacher writes on the board. In English, I'm top of the class. The girls call me 'bookworm' and giggle because I don't know about *Teen Romance*. Mom won't let me read comics.

Playing the piano for morning assembly gives me a reason to leave the classroom — I have to go to the hall to practise the hymns for tomorrow. I once heard one of the girls say she wished she could skip class. Good! I hope they're all jealous.

Our uniform — royal blue gym slip, white shirt with Peter Pan collar, striped tie, blue and white — seems to be more important than anything else. Inspection takes place every week. Prefects measure the length of our skirts as we kneel, backs straight, shoulders down. They hold their rulers upright from floor to hem. A gap wider than five inches earns a detention. So does not wearing our waist-gathered, laundry-bag knickers (they call them 'pants') and, outside the school grounds, a stupid, white Panama hat. Why?

I keep earning detention for chewing the scratchy elastic that holds the hat on from under your chin.

Even though I don't follow the rules, the teachers tell me I'm special because I can sing and play piano. The girls don't care about that. They say I won't get a boyfriend with hair like mine, all frizzy and dry — I should iron it straight, like everyone else. I tried it once. On the ironing board, with brown paper. I don't like the smell of burning hair.

I think I won't get a boyfriend because I have a flat chest, and Mom won't let me wear stockings or go to mixed parties on Saturday nights. I don't really mind. I like being at home, singing folksongs, playing guitar with Mom and Dad and my brother. On Monday mornings at school, everyone talks about who they kissed. I'm glad I stayed home — boys smell. If one of them tried to put his tongue in my mouth, I'd vomit.

One of my friends is Thembi. She sits on the grassy verge outside our school, selling fruit with her mother. And singing. Some afternoons, walking home, I join them. They can speak English, but I can't speak Zulu. Lena didn't know English or Zulu — only her own clicky language, which I didn't know, and Afrikaans, which I did. I think I still do, though sometimes I feel like it's disappeared.

Thembi has taught me how to sing Zulu songs. I love singing together in harmony — we each take a different voice, she the high note, I the low — beautiful lullaby songs, like *Thula Thula*, which I think means the same as *Lamtietie Damtietie*, but not with the same tune or rhythm. I haven't seen anyone here who looks like Lena. Dad says there aren't any Khoisan people in this part of the country. I wish we could go to the desert to find her.

Once, I took Thembi into our school building, to use the toilet. 'You can't bring her in here — tell her to use the one at the garage.'

You're not supposed to have black friends here. Black people live in rooms outside, at the back of white people's houses. Their job is to look after white people: clean their houses, cook their food, make their beds, wash and iron their clothes, look after their children, call them 'Madam' and 'Master'. Black grownups are called 'the boy' and 'the girl'. When I say I make my own bed, no one believes me, white or black. Everyone makes their own bed in England. And everywhere else I've been. Except in hotels, where I've never been, but I've heard about.

No one here knows much about England — April daffodils, rainy summers, the smell of burning leaves in the park in Autumn, Christmas in winter. And snow. None of my new friends at school has even SEEN snow! Or TV! They don't know what Beefeaters are and think that London Bridge has actually fallen down.

They also had no idea what happened inside our Johannesburg house.

Microphones planted in lights and bookshelves, policemen hiding in trees in our garden, telephones tapped — we could hear the clicking — and late at night, silent flow of people with rucksacks. Our home was a safe-house for people fighting Apartheid — people who needed to skip the country, a pillion ride, or a place beneath a sack on the back of a truck, across the border to Mozambique or Rhodesia. We never spoke about that to a single soul — black people weren't allowed in white homes unless they were 'servants'. And then only with special permits. You could end up in jail, like Mom's cousin, locked up for nine years. Or dead. Mysterious 'accidents' happened, like 'falling' from 10th-floor windows of highly secure prisons.

By the time I left high school at sixteen, a deep sense of purpose far outweighed the fear and confusion wrought by stepping on minefields of racist oppression. My brave parents showed me True North.

Some people think sixteen is too young to start university. For me, the two-year age gap is perfect. The boys in my class are just the right age. Most of them want to kiss me. Some of them have.

Bachelor of Arts in English Literature, an excuse made in heaven to do what I love — read, read, read. And march in the street, thousands of students, singing in protest.

Men in khaki with batons and tear gas tackled us down to the ground, dragged us like garbage into the backs of Black Mariahs, police vans. At John Vorster Square jail, young, Afrikaans policemen smirked as we pulled down our pants to pee in open toilets. One of them tried to touch me — I kicked him — he swore about white girls who hang out with black boys at concerts — oh yes, they knew about us — me and all my 'non-white' musician friends.

Godspell, Broadway musical hit, has thrown us together. Our mixed-race, South African cast, leaping on stage each night in Lesotho — the tiny, landlocked, but independent, black African country — is an act of defiance. In South Africa, white supremacists ruling the country have banned the show on the grounds that dancing and singing the story of Jesus is blasphemy, fated to take us all to the fires of Hell.

It also so happens that 'crossing the colour bar' — sharing a beach, or a bench, even a doorway, never mind a stage — is a crime. We in the cast all know the government ban has little to do with insulting God, but much to do with racial mixing. We might be cast out of our homeland, but we won't be stopped from singing and dancing the truth of it all.

Today my mind is off our nightly performance. High in the mountains, it's swipe and splinter of silver and white, veining a purple sky. Clash electric, metal on metal. The hills are heaving, black and lime green. I'm on a rock on the edge of the Maletsyane Falls, eating cherries. And here comes the scent — and rumble of growling bull — and water — a full-throated, African, thunder and lightning storm.

Through a break in the mist, a Basotho pony. The scrawny young boy on its back stares, as if at a ghost, at my yellow hair. I can tell it's the first time he's seen a person who looks like me. The old man behind him drops his own gaze — a sign of respect. Thousands of years ago, hunter-gatherers lived here, but none of these mountain people look like Lena.

The show was a grand success. Pouring across the border, white South Africans fought for a place in the front row, seeking the thrill of forbidden touch. Instead, they found Jesus dressed as a clown, disciples dancing and singing a story of love and betrayal. For some, Trish McKenna bouncing on Cocky Tlhotlhalemaje's lap was proof of insult to God. But no one found sex. Well, not on stage. From our side of the footlights, we couldn't tell who was who, which didn't matter — packed to the rafters for nearly three years, they whooped and clapped as one.

Why are brown people called Black? Pink people called White? People the colour of biscuits called Coloured? Why is it called the 'Immorality Act' when black and white people kiss and have sex? What happens to you when falling in love with the mixed-race, double bass player is breaking the law, and you have to pretend you don't touch?

Living together was a crime and sinful, though not before God. God didn't care, the government did — we'd go to jail for sharing a bed.

Bed which emptied of loving. Loving which drained every moment. Moment which turned to thread. Thread which sparked life when we thought we were dead.

I can't live here. I can't.

Boston, Massachusetts, USA (1976-1984)

Flamboyant coppers and golds of New England fall are bleaching pearl grey. Arctic bones finger through drape of afternoon sun, the sidewalk will soon be an ice-walk.

We'll be well below zero for months to come.

They said I'd never fall pregnant naturally — maybe not even un-naturally. Yet, here I am, properly, naturally pregnant — in a strange country, halfway through my PhD. We're clinging to shadows and echoes of African nights undercover. Shadows turning to shards. Echoes fading to out. We're pinned to the edge of no return.

Divine justice, once-in-a-lifetime-chance to bear a child. I'm doing this joyously, with or without him.

Chlorophyl dies as temperature drops. Leaves change colour and fall, making way.

The PhD Teaching Fellows each have an office. We all have corkboards festooned with photos and postcards from home. M, from the Bronx in New York, writing her thesis on women's shelters, is spitting with rage about my photos of black, bare-breasted, beaded women, traditional Zulu dancers.

'How would *you* feel if *I* hung pictures of naked *white* women on *my* office wall?'

'M, it's not what you think...'

'Then what?'

'They're African dancers...'

'You mean they're not exploitative porn?'

Part of me wants to scoop her into my arms — born of humans traded, grafted, implanted, her gaze supplanted by those who ripped her from Africa's belly, M is a blinded baby who's lost her Mother.

'It's traditional dress.'

'Say what you like — bare tits are bare tits.'

Bile rising, we're both infected — both colonised, mutants. Impotent, dumb, I drown her in echoes of African harmonies riding on thunder, bulls growling, stillness of faraway plateaus of dry, yellow grass and red sand.

At home, a biscuit-brown man slouches against the window, watching me pack, eyes yellow, unblinking. He was my life. Now I can't utter his name.

Outside, monochrome, mostly black. Minus five. Fahrenheit.

'Why such a small case?'

'I'll only be gone for a month.'

Face dead. He hasn't heard me. Sound fogs when you're digging tunnels through ice.

At the bottom of a drawer — cocoon of underwear, scarves, sachets of dried petals — a flimsy silk bag. Treasured seashells, pink like feathers, blue like snow, from when we walked on Crane's beach, before the bruising, before the baby was born. Two, thin ribbons hang from the little sac's gaping mouth. Tie them, tie them, tie them together.

He straightens... 'Hey — what's that you're taking?' ...lithe as a cheetah. One stride. One fist. My hands fly up to cover my face. Shells scatter and chip.

'It's nothing... it's nothing.'

But that's not true. Amongst the splintered shells, one darker, earth-red, unchipped, not-shell.

Lunging forward through bloodied eyes, I swipe it up, grab my baby, fling myself barefoot out of the house. Into the freezing night.

Running, running, running, running.
Packed snow gnawing my feet to nothing, running.
Don't slip, don't slip, don't slip, for God's sake.
Running, running.
As if I know where I'm going.
And yes, I do.
I do.
Into the echo, curling like smoke from inside my hand —
between my fingers — the sound of crickets at night.
'Kom huis toe, my liefie. Kom huis toe.'/Come home my sweet-
heart, come home.
Wrapped round my child, clutching my Kalahari *klip*, I squeeze
my frozen eyes tight, and leap.

RETURN

We land in a pool of yellow grass.
The dusty scent of a coming storm.
A humming.
'Lamtietjie, damtietjie, doo-doo-doo...'
Just ahead, on a mound of red earth, a *bokkie*, legs the colour of
biscuits.
I hold my baby girl out to Lena and turn my face to the rain.

POWERED BY 4

LIVING WITH THE WALL

FENNA WILLIAMS

6.07 am. The Paris-Moscow-Express screeches to a halt on the viaduct opposite my bedroom window. Who needs an alarm clock when there are brakes on a train that has barely been serviced since the Wall was built? I lie in bed until the red signal is lifted and imagine the journey the passengers have in front of them. No matter where they come from, they all need a visa to go any further. It's only one short mile from my house to *Bahnhof Friedrichstraße*, the first station in Berlin-East, but there is a border in between with watch towers, fences with automatic shooting devices, land mines and patrol guards with dogs, guns and a firing order for anyone violating it.

While the train crosses the Iron Curtain, I get up and into the shower to start my day in a city cut into four pieces like a cake. I live in the British slice, go shopping in the French one and attend university in the American, while my family and friends live in the Soviet Sector, known as East Berlin. If this proves to be a good day and my visa comes through, I will take one of the trains that pass my window and meet them in the evening.

It is 1986, and, as every morning for the past four years, I walk my dog along the train tracks. His name is Bukfenc, Hungarian for 'somersault', because he tumbled out of a friend's car from

Budapest when I first got him, a Bobtail ball of fur. Bukfenc always leads the way, as he knows where and what we are heading for.

At the end of my street, we turn right and enter a kind of no man's land after crossing the river Spree, which flows between my house and the Berlin Wall. This was my city's heart and soul, the former centre of town, before it was divided by a concrete barrier. No houses remain, apart from one. The Swiss Embassy stands out in the void, like the last tooth in an otherwise empty mouth that has lost its power to speak.

I am not afraid to walk along the Wall in solitude, as watchful eyes are upon me at all times from the Eastern side. I am both targeted and protected by the men observing my every step from their lookout. I wave to them out of pity. They guard the *Todesstreifen*, the death strip, and they guard each other, never allowed to be on duty with the same man twice, to prevent bonding. They know they will have to shoot anyone trying to cross the frontier illegally, including their own comrades, were any of them to try to reach my side.

In all the years walking this path, I have never seen any of them in conversation but caught them looking intensely at every conceivable diversion. My dog never disappoints them. As there are no trees around, he runs towards the Wall at full speed, then cocks his leg, peeing gleefully against history.

Berliners have developed a similar attitude to the life they lead. We stoically ignore the fact that we are the Cold War's buffer zone and ruled by the Four Power Agreement[1]. We try to make the best out of every sector's peculiarities, celebrating French or American fairs or visiting a Tattoo in the Olympic stadium, presented by the Scottish regiments stationed in the city. I attend every event without fail, for they are the icing on the Quadripartite cake that grants us

---

1. Official text of the Quadripartite Agreement, see: United States Department of State. Documents on Germany 1944-1985. Washington: Department of State [s.d.]. 1421 p. (Department of State Publication 9446). p. 1135-1143. http://www.cvce.eu/obj/quadripartite_agreement_on_berlin_berlin_3_september_1971-en-9bfcb5f5-8e0d-46ee-9f7f-8e9a7c945fa7.html

the freedom we cherish, and which we put to the test with more peace demonstrations, squatted houses and political activities than any other place in the Germanies.

Twenty-five years after the Wall has fallen, I sit in Edinburgh Castle for my first 'real' Tattoo, happily humming and singing along to every song. A couple in the row before me, their tartan attire giving them away as Scots, keep turning their heads when they hear my husband and me converse in the rather unmistakable Berlin accent. During the interval, the lady, about ten years my junior, turns to me: 'Are you from Berlin?'

As I nod, she introduces herself as Margaret and adds, in a mixture of German and Scots: 'I used to live in Spandau.'

I put her to the test by answering: 'Oh, for a moment there I thought we were from the same city!'

Even though the city of Spandau became part of Berlin as early as 1920, the inhabitants still claim to live *near* the big sister instead of being just a part of it, thereby proudly pointing out their own heritage.

Margaret laughed heartily at my inside joke. 'I loved the distinction. It reflected the illusion of a normal life in which you could drive from one city to the next to visit each other.'

I agreed. It gave room to breathe where there was restriction everywhere, either by some seventy-five miles of fortified border to East Germany or because of twenty-eight miles of Wall that divided the inner city's two ventricles.

Margaret's father was with the Gordon Highlanders and part of the Tattoo I treasured, playing the bagpipes. A haunting air on a bagpipe seemed to me the ultimate sound for my city at the time: not quite in tune with other instruments but piercing through to my core, pulling at my heartstrings because I would never be able to experience the Tattoo together with my family and friends from the Eastern side.

Germans and Celtic people have a sentiment in common that only a few languages can express in one word. *Sehnsucht* and *hiraeth* share the same bittersweet longing for something that might even be too big to wish for. *Sehnsucht* is never judging, never angry, just keeping the hope alive that you can one day be complete, united with your missing pieces.

My missing pieces are called Donata, Georg, Anett, Hilda, Erich, Melitta and Hermann. My substitute for completeness is travelling and getting to know other cultures. Cultures that share my sentiments and cultures that teach me how to live without them and survive.

'Bagpipes, Gaelic, kilts, music by Runrig and single malt whisky,' I admit to my new acquaintances in Edinburgh Castle. 'The Tattoo made me fall in love with anything Scottish.'

Margaret lists what she loved about Berlin — and I fall for her, too, because in her time there she came to understand my city, cherished what we cherished.

'*Currywurst, Berliner Weiße*, the abundance of rivers, lakes and waterways and the get-on-with-it-despite-lifestyle.' Margaret giggles. 'Nowhere else did people walk down the street to a bottle bank to save resources. Our house stood next to one of them. As Berlin was constantly celebrating something, it was used any time of day — and night.'

While following Bukfenc on to the Reichstag and the Brandenburg Gate, I can hear almost all languages this globe has on offer. Nearly everyone visiting Berlin comes here, either to have their picture taken in front of the Wall with the famous monument in the background, or to climb the viewing platforms for a closer look. That is why my dog and I do what I call our 'history round' as early in the morning as possible, before the tourist buses pour out spectators by the hundreds.

'A brief glimpse does not allow for insights,' I remind everyone I take here myself, either privately or in my job as a tour guide. I recommend they all visit the Soviet sector at least once.

My friends and family in East Berlin are as much part of my life as if they lived next door. The very different interpretation of the Four Power Status in the largest of the sectors has a massive influence on our daily life. I feel put on a leash when I cross the border, chained to a collar that is at best invisible but can choke painfully if the authorities decide to play games by denying me entry at the very last moment. There is no doubt who is in control.

Donata is the best friend I have in East Berlin. I can visit her, but she will never be permitted to stay with me. She is my age, has two kids and a husband who takes care of them when we girls have our monthly night out. Donata is fearless when it comes to the forbidden so-called 'contact with the West'. If spending time with me means she will not be promoted in her socialist company manufacturing chemical products, she shrugs her shoulders. 'Life is not made for work,' she says, 'but to make life work.' We share the same taste in almost everything, and where it differs, it feels like a welcome completion.

Karat is the band we dig. The lyrics to their songs are poetic as well as a great singalong and undercover political statement. For years Donata and I have been waiting for a concert we can attend together. Finally, on one of our First-Wednesday-of-the-month-meetings she waves small pieces of paper when I arrive at her doorstep.

'Tickets for Karat! Eight tickets for Karat! Martin got hold of them,' she shouts.

We waltz around her flat. Giddy with joy, we make plans for the big day. I promise to bring slush money. 'The exchange rate is 1:10 now. Fifty Deutschmark will buy us 500 *Ostmark* and an unforgettable evening. You do the shopping; I'll bring the money for the after-show blast.'

Donata has more good news. 'Martin and Jenny have offered their new flat for the event. It is close to the concert hall. They are practically living in the ticket office.'

'Martin must have queued four times to get us all in,' I answer.

Due to public demand, the ticket counter only hands out two tickets per sale. I am impressed by his commitment to our circle of friends and promise to buy him Scottish Whisky in the *Intershop*, the Duty-Free facility at the border, to show our appreciation.

'By the way, it looks as if we can congratulate Jenny and Martin. The adoption papers are through. Seven years of waiting and now they've finally been promised a child.'

'Karat must have written their hit just for them,' I say and, like teenagers instead of nearly thirty-year-old women, we sing into imaginary microphones:

'*Über 7 Brücken musst du gehn*/You need to cross 7 bridges
7 dunkle Jahre überstehn/endure 7 dark ages
7 mal wirst du die Asche sein/7 times you will burn to ashes
Aber einmal auch der helle Schein/to one day rise as shining light.'[2]

As my dog and I turn away from the Wall and walk South towards the Soviet War Memorial, I start humming the Karat tune. The melancholy text seems strangely appropriate for this part of my daily promenade.

I always put Bukfenc on a leash while we pass the Russian honour guards who stand firm, even in the wind and the rain, paying tribute to some 2000 Red Army soldiers buried behind them and a further 80,000 who died during the Battle of Berlin between April and May 1945. It is a comforting thought that this memorial was erected in the British sector and the building of it agreed on by

---

2. ÜBER SIEBEN BRÜCKEN MUSST DU GEHN
   Music: Ulrich Swillms
   Lyrics: Helmut Richter
   © 1980 by Harth Musik Verlag GmbH
   with kind permission:
   ROBA MusiK Verlag GmbH
   Translation in this text by the author
   German version: https://www.youtube.com/watch?v=7lgTu-v55s0

all Allied Powers. If they settled around a table back then, they might do it again one day to negotiate Berlin's fate. Germany's fate. Mine.

I once walked past here with my penfriend Priscilla from South Africa. Priscilla was distraught by the walk along the death strip and the imbalance of Soviet power versus the other three forces. 'How can you live with this as if it is normal?'

'I can, because there is a difference between normality and reality. Normality is what we long for, reality is what we try to face and get on with.'

Priscilla agreed and talked about Apartheid in her country. Both of us were becoming gloomier with every step, until my penfriend asked: 'What would be the most incredible, the most beautiful thing that could happen to you in your city?'

I didn't have to think about it. 'I dream about walking towards Brandenburg Gate to meet Donata. I imagine us coming towards each other — one from the East and one from the West — meeting inside the Gate, and far and away, no Wall, no border guard bearing down on us. I dream about Brandenburg Gate being a gate again.'

Priscilla liked the picture but thought it as unlikely as I did. 'Applied to South Africa, that would mean white and black people join hands, eventually even accepting a coloured president,' she said. 'I guess you would call that Utopia, and add to it, 'Dream on!'

Bukfenc and I now reach our favourite part of the walk, the *Tiergarten*, Berlin's largest landscape garden, twice the size of Central Park, New York. I veer to the right to enjoy the flowerbeds, the abundance of trees, the waters of the river Spree and the peace. We are right in the centre of town, but all I hear is birdsong and the rustling of treetops all the way down to Bellevue Palace. The stately home is the residence of the president of the Federal Republic of Germany when he is visiting the city. A symbol of the country's connection to Berlin even though to many West Germans we are a passing thought. After all, we are twice as far away from them as from the Polish border.

Borders make up my life, especially the eight crossings between

West and East Berlin. The one at *Friedrichstraße* can teach any newcomer a thing or two about German efficiency combined with Soviet authority.

Many people feel intimidated by the semi-dark, claustrophobic rooms barely wide enough for one person, with doors that only open if somebody you never see presses a button. I take everything in my stride and nod to the person behind the bullet-proof glass, handing over my green provisional identity card[3] which permits me to stay over until 2 o'clock at night, thirty times a year.

'Turn your face to the side and show your left ear!'

I do as the border guard orders and dutifully turn my head, thereby looking at the narrow steel door that stands between me and my plans for the evening. My opponent is young, about ten years my junior, his hair a tiny bit longer than normally tolerated in this job.

Above me sits the mirror that allows him to scan me from head to toe. When I look up, I see that he is scrutinizing my identity card and the visa I brought. He takes his time to compare my looks with the photo in the documents and counts the entry stamps on my visa card several times.

'Last trip for you today,' says the man with the power to deny me entrance and spoil my day.

'For this year, yes.'

I am astonished by how he worded his sentence. The end of the year is near, naturally I am through with my visas. If this is not his first day in this position, he knows that for all except private purposes I use one of my semi-legal passports from West-Germany[4] issued to addresses I have never lived at and don't intend to, adopting the letterbox company principle. I own three of them to make sure that I can take as many tour groups as possible over the

---

3. Behelfsmäßiger Ausweis: provisional identity card for people from Berlin, naming the holder a German national, rather than a German as done in a West German passport.
4. Reisepass der Bundesrepublik Deutschland, the bearer of this passport is a German.

border and still have my First-Wednesday-of-the-Month meetings with Donata. An arrangement like the one I have with her is necessary, as contact by telephone is next to impossible due to unwelcome listeners crowding the line.

'What is the purpose of your visit? Friends? Relatives?'

'Culture,' I answer. 'I am going to a concert.'

'Karat,' he says.

Our eyes lock. He is a fan, too. One that didn't get a ticket. It is only now that I realize just how extraordinary it is to hold eight.

'Who bought the ticket?' he demands to know.

'I did,' I lie. 'I queued last month.' As one can never be sure what is cooking in the political stew, I never give names in case some ingredient is no longer part of the recipe.

'Remember to be back here two hours after midnight. There are no exceptions, not tonight, not ever,' he reminds me, while he takes the money for the visa and the 25 Deutschmark compulsory exchange.

My heart pumps an additional beat when he hands back my papers. 'Customs,' he adds and points at my backpack.

The buzzer sounds and the steel door opens automatically to spit me out into the next room. Before it closes again, I hear him speak into a phone.

'Search her.' His way to cope with envy.

A woman in uniform, with decorations and medals where her heart should be, escorts me into an anteroom.

I shiver when she does not search my bag but orders me to take off my clothes. She looks at everything I hand her, even reads the washing instructions if they are still attached. When she takes my boots and rips out their insoles, I know that she is looking for the slush money I exchanged and rack my brain: who the hell told her superiors that I wanted to bring any?

Uniform can search me till hell freezes over because I have nothing forbidden on me. No newspaper clip, no tape with the latest hits from the West, not even Donata's favourite chocolate. On an impulse I handed all that to a friend who right now is driving over at Checkpoint Charlie, the black money hidden under the battery of his car.

I dress, shaking like a leaf, while I understand that this search had nothing to do with envy, but with vital information from and to the wrong places. A massive headache sets in as I try to control my breathing and keep a calm that seems forever out of reach from this day forward. I go through the list of people invited to the party and come to grips with the fact that one of them is an informant.

Uniform is visibly disappointed. That we have in common.

We also share the same mole. Her superiors know his name. I don't.

But I do know three different things:

One of my buddies waiting for me in front of the concert hall is not a friend.

The 500 Ostmark will not be used but silently end up in a bin on my way back to the *Tränenpalast*, the 'Palace of Tears', through which I will leave for home. No one is to see this money. No friend. No foe. No one is going to be questioned, no one is going to suffer for it.

Last but not least, I know I will keep my knowledge to myself tonight and let the others celebrate in style. Karat will sing and the Secret Police will most probably hear all about our evening the following day. I will weep when they play my favourite song, but I will not give the Stasi more than that.

Music can connect us to an experience and help us to remember it vividly as soon as the first chords reach our ear. For months after the concert, my Karat tapes remain untouched while my life has changed from major to minor. My daily round is more of a comfort than ever.

At a little past 7.30 am, Bukfenc and I reach the dog exercise area where we meet the same people every morning. While he is courting his favourite Afghan lady I talk to the owner. Carmen needs a dog sitter for a fortnight and my dog immediately agrees to share his second-best bed with Anouschka.

Carmen and I talk about my Karat encounter, and she warns me to stay put a little longer. 'That was a close call,' she says. 'We don't want you to be cut off from your friends and relations entirely.'

'It is a little more complicated than that,' I explain. 'I received a letter from the West Berlin police. East German authorities have declared me dead. *Deceased at border*, they state. A dead woman can't apply for a visa at all, right?'

Carmen sighs as if a naughty child has annoyed her. 'That's a new one, isn't it? What will you do now?'

'Rise from the dead with a different identity card or move to West Germany.'

'Move away? Why?' Carmen winks at me. 'We don't want to answer this folly with something that drastic, do we?'

I take my leave of her, coming full circle by turning into my street right after the train's viaduct. One hundred paces later I see him. Under the oak tree that shades my house, Martin is waiting for me.

'I was the first to cross the border this morning,' he says, as if he has done it before and a visit from an East Berliner in the West is bordering on normal.

'Who died?' I ask, because that's the only reason I know why someone his age is let out of the cage under the condition that he has a spouse and child waiting at home as a pawn.

'My aunt was ill for months,' he says. 'I have seventy-two hours to arrange the funeral and sell her flat. Which I won't.'

'I see,' I say. And I do. He is not going back.

'Jenny and the little one are fine, devoted to each other. They will cope,' he defends himself, even though I did not ask about them.

I close my eyes because a wave of pity washes over me thinking of those two on the other side of the border. They will suffer severely for his freedom.

'Are you not afraid of getting lonely?' I ask.

'Here?' Martin shakes his head. 'No way. If you turn your back on me, I'll make friends with the Eiffel Tower in Paris, the Colosseum in Rome and the taste of freedom in my mouth.'

I try to understand. Freedom within sight, but still out of reach, is particularly hard to bear. I see that every time I say goodbye to Donata at the Palace of Tears, which has earned its name for bitter reasons.

'You planned this carefully,' I say, as suddenly everything falls into place. Knowing his aunt was ill, Martin wanted to make sure he would have this one chance to leave East Berlin by playing a good socialist, who would earn himself a child and a day in the West by spying on us. 'How long did this go on? Did you have to tell them much?'

He remains silent.

'At least we all got Karat tickets for the price you paid,' I say. All the other questions I have, he will not be able to answer, as no one knows what the secret police knits out of the information they get.

I take Martin into my house. He has a hard time ahead, even without me judging him. He is a GDR refugee now, one that can never go back without vanishing into one of the darkest prisons Europe has on offer.

Three years later, on 9th November 1989, Karat's Seven-Bridges-Song is played everywhere, as the last bridge is crossed, the seven dark ages history, the Wall gone. The song is my *Sehnsucht* fulfilled, my *hiraeth* palpable through every note.

By midnight New Year's Eve, 1990, my passport gets stamped for the very last time. Donata and I meet inside the Brandenburg Gate, and I can take her home to my flat at long last.

The Allied Forces sit around a table and talk. And, finally, on 3rd October 1990, they hand their power to a united Germany.

Now I could read my Stasi file.

More than thirty years on, I still haven't done that. It was a matter of luck that I could walk my dog on the free side of the Wall. But who knows how I would have lived otherwise? Would they have broken me early on? Would I have joined their forces with pride?

It is hard enough to live with some of the memories, no need to uncover other people's shame to top that. I'd rather collect good ones by going on holiday with my friends, cheering the freedom we now own. Freedom to travel, freedom to love anyone we want and freedom of the mind. The ultimate *Sehnsucht*, the missing pieces that can complete anyone.

As a final act of their influence on my life, the Four Powers have granted me the utopia Priscilla and I believed would never come. I hope I don't need to leave it. Not now, not ever. And so, I pray that the Paris-Moscow-Express, suspended since the 24th of February 2022 due to another war raging in Europe, gets the green signal of peace to pass my house again at 6:07 every morning.

Glossary:

Bahnhof- train station.

Berliner Weisse- a pale, top-fermented beer with 3% alcohol, usually drunk with a shot of woodruff- or raspberry-sirup.

Brandenburger Tor- The Brandenburg Gate was built in the late 18th century as a representative gate to the then Prussian Berlin. It formed the Western end of the magnificent boulevard 'Unter den Linden' that leads directly to Alexanderplatz with famous buildings of the era to the left and right. It became the city's landmark and was inaccessible to the public while the Wall was standing, as it was located directly behind the border in the Soviet sector. Neither East- nor West-Berliners were able to come near, let alone walk through it.

Bottle banks- as Berliners had to be careful with their resources due to the 'island situation', they collected and recycled as much as they could. Bottle banks were introduced at the beginning of the 1970s.

Checkpoint Charlie- was the border crossing between the US and the Soviet sector in divided Berlin. It was also the official crossing for military personnel, diplomats and officials of the Federal Republic of Germany, who were not searched here. The name derives from the NATO alphabet: A for Alpha was the crossing point from the FRG into the German Democratic Republic at Helmstedt, Checkpoint Bravo the one you took when leaving the GDR after travelling the transit route to West-Berlin in Drewitz and Checkpoint Charlie the one leading back into the East once you drove all the way through West Berlin.

Currywurst- right after the war, a woman named Herta Heuwer from Berlin had the idea to combine a sausage from Spandau with her special seasoning sauce made from tomatoes and curry and to sell this from her own food stall. An early kind of fast food that turned into one of the most popular exports from Berlin to both Germanies.

Intershop- retail shops that were found in large hotels and near border crossings as well as on the transit routes. Shopping in these stores was only possible against payment in foreign currency. Consequently, they were not much used by GDR inhabitants. Prices, especially for alcoholic beverages, were much lower than in the FRG. The Intershops therefore functioned as a kind of duty-free zone. Intershops were set up to earn as much hard currency for Eastern Germany as possible.

Karat- an East German rock band that was famous in the East as well as in the West and is still wowing audiences today.

Paris-Moscow-Express- it takes 22h and 28m to travel from Berlin to Moscow, or 39h and 33m for the entire route from Paris.

Reichstag- housed a permanent exhibition on German history when I did my dog walks but became the seat of the German Bundestag after unification. The first session took place on October 4th 1990, one day after the Four Allies had handed their power over to a combined parliament of the West German Bundestag and the East German Volkskammer.

Schloss Bellevue- Bellevue Palace is still used for receptions by the German Federal President, but he now lives in Villa Wurmbach in Berlin-Dahlem

Tiergarten- is the name of the city district where I lived as well as the name of the largest inner-city park which borders onto Berlin Mitte, the old and new centre of Berlin

Todesstreifen- literally translated: band of death. The layout of the death strip underwent constant changes. By 1989 it was between 15 and 150m wide depending on the geographical situation. It had a 23m 'Hinterland barrier fence' and beyond that a 2m high 'contact signal fence'. Parallel to this, dogs were chained to a running system that made them stay within the track but allowed them to guard otherwise blind spots. Additionally, there was a section of observation towers and earth bunkers, all of them brightly illuminated all night. The last section before the wall was built like a kind of vehicle barrier ditch. The end of that barrier consisted of a 3.50-4.00m high and at least 10cm thick wall, sometimes with barbed wire on top, sometimes with a kind of pipe, too round for the human grip. One would slide off every time one wanted to get a hold to climb over.

Between 1961 and 1989 at least 140 people died at the Berlin Wall. The last one was shot on 5th February 1989.

Zwangsumtausch- compulsory exchange of 25 DM or its equivalent was required from anyone wanting to visit East Berlin or East Germany. With millions of people crossing over every year to see their relatives and friends, this money helped the GDR survive as long as it did. While the exchange rate at the border was 1:1, international banks paid far more. Therefore, buying slush money was common amongst the Westerners, some even exchanging it directly in East Berlin with friends who needed hard currency. Nevertheless, having black money on you or a lot of foreign currency was a criminal offence in the GDR. You would be

suspected of using the money for purposes such as trying to get
somebody out to the West or trying to corrupt somebody.

Bibliography

Der Senator für Wirtschaft und Arbeit Berlin (Hrsg): *Berlin, eine
Stadt zum Leben und Arbeiten, Wissenswertes von A bis Z, Nach-
schlagewerk*, Berlin 1985
Elefanten Press, Irene Lusk, Christiane Zieseke, *Stadtfront Berlin
Frontstadt Berlin West Berlin*, Elefanten Press Verlag GmbH,
Berlin 1982
Informationszentrum Berlin, Ernst Luuk (Hrgb): *Berlin – Im
Überblick, Schrift zur 750 Jahrfeier der Stadt*, Berlin 1987
Karl Heinz Gehm, Wolfgang Kruse: *Berlin in Brief*, Presse- und
Informationsamt des Landes Berlin, English Version of the 14th
German edition by Joan Glenn, Berlin 1982
Merian Berlin kompakt + Merian Extra Hauptstadt Berlin, Hoff-
mann und Campe Verlag, Hamburg 13. September 1991
Spaziergänge zu Industrie und Technik Nr. 4, herausgegeben vom
Presse- und Informationsamt des Landes Berlin, Berlin 1983
Theodor Müller-Alfeld (Hrsg): *Berlin gestern und heute*, Lizenzaus-
gabe des Stapp Verlages, Wolfgang Stapp, Berlin für Bertelsmann,
Gütersloh
Quadripartite Agreement on Berlin: Signed in Berlin on 3rd
September 1971 by representatives from France, the United
Kingdom of Great Britain and Northern Ireland, the United States
of America and the USSR, the Quadripartite Agreement on Berlin
marks a relaxation of tension in East-West relations, in particular
since it guarantees civil communications between West Berlin and
the Federal Republic of Germany (FRG).
Source: United States Department of State. Documents on

Germany 1944-1985. Washington: Department of State [s.d.]. 1421 p. (Department of State Publication 9446). p. 1135-1143.
Copyright: United States of America Department of State;
http://www.cvce.eu/obj/quadripartite_agreement_on_berlin_berlin_3_september_1971-en-9bfcb5f5-8e0d-46ee-9f7f-8e9a7c945-fa7.html
Last updated: 03/07/2015

Dedicated to everyone who survived those times with the help of friends and relatives – and Karat's music.

CRUSH

CANDY SMELLIE

M y first crush was unobtainable, destined never to last. Virgil Tracy's good looks and cool head in a crisis attracted me from the very beginning. There were of course strings attached. Literally, in his case, as he was a puppet from the television programme *Thunderbirds*. I'm not sure the creators could've predicted these puppets' effect on me (and probably others, though I never found any). Not for me the chiselled visage of Scott, or the weird John who spent all his time in space on Thunderbird Five. Gordon could swim, which came in handy as they lived on an island. And finally, Alan who was in love with Tin Tin, though you never saw them hold hands (tricky manoeuvre for puppeteers, I later discovered).

No, it was Virgil in Thunderbird Two who had my tender heart. He flew this huge green beast of an aircraft which could pick up and deliver all the equipment needed — Demolition Canon, Heat-proof Rescue Cage, or Heavy-duty Electromagnetic Grabs — to perform the rescue operations they were called to. Thirty-two episodes worth of heavy lifting.

It didn't matter how many times Valerie Singleton[1] extolled the virtues of 'build it yourself', I could not be cajoled into making my own Tracy Island, regardless of how many loo rolls and sticky-backed plastic sheets I'd hoarded.

However, Virgil was not the first puppet I noticed, oh dear me, no. You must remember that this was the era of early kids TV. Up until this point, the only diversion we had from making dens in the living room or chasing next door's dog, was *Muffin the Mule* or *Listen with Mother* on the radio. My mother was keen on neither, but she also disliked the next door's dog, so I was onto a loser there.

The first of the 'new' marionettes came from outer space (i.e., the USA) via the aptly named *Space Patrol*. Never produced in colour, we had to make up our own minds on what they would have looked like. Slim was a Venusian and obviously had to be blue. Further investigations into memory indicated that this was incorrect, and though strangely 'craniumed', he was pink. My nine-year-old head found him weird but, in a way hard to diagnose, I just found him attractive.

In practical terms, *Thunderbirds* was the brainchild of Gerry and Sylvia Anderson who together invented something they called 'Supermarionation', which allowed the puppeteers to work with scaled models and part electronic marionettes. They developed many programmes during the 1960s, but it was *Thunderbirds* that really grabbed the imagination. There was a live action film based on the characters — too late for me by this time, but it was interesting to see how they'd developed.

Recollections are a bit hazy at this remove, but it seemed at the time that the boys in my class didn't demonstrate the same passion for distant and unreachable objects as I and my girlfriends did. Asking my male friends now suggests this observation is correct. Boys just weren't that interested until, that is, they had a crush on

1. Valerie Singleton is an English television and radio personality best known as a regular presenter of the popular children's series *Blue Peter* from 1962 to 1972.

someone in the class or the girl down the street. For many of them these were just as unobtainable.

And so, I moved on to my next crush.

Virgil was supplanted in my affections by Illya Kuryakin, no more attainable. Yes, he had a heartbeat, which was a step up, but he was a spy played by an actor in the TV show of *Man from Uncle*. Thursday nights had never been so eagerly awaited by this 10-year-old. At 7:30, *Top of the Pops* (TOPs)[2] was on the telly. We would gather round to guess number one that week — in September 1964, it was 'House of the Rising Sun' by The Animals.

Many may recall Sunday evenings spent pressing 'record-stop-record' on cassette tape players. TOPs was absolutely required listening, or you would have nothing to discuss at school on Monday morning. The cool kids were gathering around to discuss *Monty Python*[3], but my parents deemed this unsuitable so TOPs it was.

TOPs will be forever linked to the first time I watched *Man from Uncle*. I couldn't believe my eyes; here was someone simply divine. Blond of hair and light of eye. We only had black and white TV, so I admit to using my imagination here. And to being instantly in love. Each week I would be breathless with anticipation for the sound of the Radio Times landing on the doormat. Would he be in it this week? Were they on the cover? Could there be a colour image? To me, he was completely unrelated to the actor David McCallum. My friend Rachel and I would spend hours in my room creating stories and short plays based on the characters.

There's a part of me now that thinks maybe Rachel's heart

---

2. Distinctly different from the Sunday night Top 20 show on Radio and competing for listeners with the pirate ships anchored off the coast of Essex.
3. Monty Python was a bit like the curate's egg in that there were streaks of brilliance interspersed with the direst apology for humour. I will however have no criticism for The Life of Brian, still the best movie of all time.

wasn't quite as committed as mine. Now, of course, the stories we wrote would be described as *fanfic*,[4] so we were very early adopters of this modern trend. I must own up: I would insist Rachel play Napoleon Solo to my Illya without any recourse to state her preference. We'd found an abandoned house in the village and would play spies on our way home from school. Rachel would, however, refuse to run around the garden brandishing fake guns. Some friend!

31st December 1966 was the first time The Monkees were seen on UK TV, and I was there, glued to the small screen in my Nana's house, wondering if I would ever be able to breath normally again. My world was knocked sideways as I fell for Davy Jones. Warm-blooded and real, though no more obtainable, he changed the world of this pre-teen.

Prior to this point, there were bands to worship of course but somehow The Monkees were different. Davy was one of four members of an anarchic 'fake' band that included Mike Nesmith,[5] Mickey Dolenz and Peter Tork, created by TV executives in Hollywood. This was the first time young people were seen living apart from their families. If you grew up watching *The Brady Bunch* or *Bewitched*, or even *The Addams Family*, then teenagers all lived with their families, even if, in the latter's case, they tried to kill each other!

Such was the extreme response from the fans that these four young men began to demand they perform their songs in concert, playing their own instruments. Tricky in Davy's case, as he couldn't play anything, but as far as I was concerned, he could stand in a tub of baked beans blowing a kazoo and I would adore him.

---

4. First appeared as 'fan fiction' in 1939 about predominately male amateur science fiction. The author would borrow unauthorised copyrighted characters in existing works and base stories around them.

5. Mike Nesmith is credited with creating the first music-only TV channel, leading to the start of MTV. His mother Bette invented Liquid Paper correction fluid for use on typed documents, invaluable to the clumsy typist.

The band had some extraordinary writers on the team, songs that to this day fill many a karaoke evening. 'I'm a Believer' was written by Neil Diamond, and 'Pleasant Valley Sunday', by Gerry Goffin and Carole King. There were many more. Their album sales on the back of the TV series brought in millions, and 'merch'[6] became something that girls sought.

Twelve and worldly-wise in the art of the crush, I was not able to bring Rachel with me this time, but found many others who were equally besotted. Acquiring posters, magazines and books, music and keepsakes — I was busily in love, every waking minute of the day. So much so that schoolwork was ignored, to the detriment of my parents' ambitions. The end-of-year report card was so bad that to this day it's still marked with the tears of my mother's despair. Her only recourse was to tear down every assiduously garnered poster. Even now the memory stings. Years later she had no recollection of this act of vandalism.

Rachel and I (yes, the same Rachel who wouldn't play Man from Uncle) became more than mildly obsessed with the *Whiteoaks of Jalna* by Mazo de la Roche. Not sure that these books are still in print, but our local library had all sixteen of them and we devoured every one. Each step that this family took, we wanted to emulate.

We imagined we were the aged Aunt who never left her room, never ate a meal, and yet somehow became so vast she was unable to move, though further into the books we discovered she was secretly fed trays of food by the servants. Or we were Finch, who was delicate and played the piano. We saw him as a tragic, consumptive, Chopin-like figure, collapsing over the blood-stained keys but manfully playing on. Our imagination flew off the scrappy notebooks we shared, taking turns to write a 'chapter'. And yes, I

---

6. Merch (merchandise), popular in the music industry, raises revenue for bands and their management.

suppose I imagined myself married to Finch and saving him from the disease that, in the books, eventually killed him.

Then there was the boy at the bus stop at the end of our road. He wouldn't have known anything of the care and attention I would give to my school uniform (a drab grey that suited no one) or of the attempt to leave the house with mascara. My dad would drive me to school. I never did ask him if he noticed my weird behaviour. We would roll up our skirts creating a thick wad of material under the waistband in an attempt to look cool sporting a mini-skirt, something I don't believe any teen ever achieved. All traces of make-up were removed prior to the start of the school day, judiciously reapplied for the bus ride home after.

On the way to thirteen, I discovered the Bee Gees. Unlike most of my friends who had their eyes on the Brothers Gibb, I'd set my sight on their guitarist, Vince Maloney. For some reason, he stirred in me a passion for rock and pop music that The Monkees hadn't. So much so that I started writing about him falling ill in a hotel corridor and having to nurse him back to life. This is a thing now, something that people write about in numerous fanfic pages on the internet.

Every one of my crushes was like a heartbeat, and distinctly superior to my first real boyfriend who caused my beating heart to flatline. Uncomfortable to dip into this memory but it must be done. I met No Name on an evening out at the local dance spot in Cambridge.

The Dorothy Dance Hall was the place to be, and every Saturday evening that's where we sixteen-year-olds flocked, like exotic ne'er-do-wells pretending to be bad boys. This was the era of the skinhead but before the emergence of punk rock (regarded as an argument against new romantics). We tried to conform, to be seen wearing the right clothes. Honestly, it was a tightrope we all tottered along on an evening out.

In my case it was a Ben Sherman shirt, two-toned, stay-pressed trousers, and huge shoes. Hair was supposed to be very short on top, long and straight at the back. Mullets were all the rage in 1970. With my bonce of badly behaved curls and enormous head, I looked like an overstuffed lollipop on steroids wearing plant pots for boots. Utterly ridiculous, but reluctant to admit it.

No Name also frequented the Dorothy and was impressively cool. When he asked me to dance, I was immediately jumping — both physically and mentally. This was real. I was there with a boy and my friends could see me. The respect this generated from my peers was immense. But it all went wrong on New Year's Eve, again at the Dorothy, when he joyfully told me that he'd only asked me to dance as a dare from his pals to find the ugliest girl in the place and ask her out.

I was crushed, devastated, miserable. I didn't eat for weeks (slight exaggeration, but even now I can remember that knot in my stomach that refused anything other than water). Just how could anyone do this to another person. Where was the delicious sweetness of my pre-teen crushes?

I'm not proud to admit this, but I may have meted out some of the same punishment I'd received from the cruel mouth of No Name. I do remember that I would stand in the middle of the dance floor or bar, hold up a cigarette and see who would provide the torch. It did garner some interesting people though.

———

From the Bobby Sockers of the 1940s swooning over Frank Sinatra to today's preteens fantasising about living in South Korea with anodyne boy bands, the heart-stopping infatuation of a young girl is hard to appreciate unless you've experienced it for yourself. Crushed under the weight of feelings so vast, as if you are the only person in the world to have felt this way. And yet the subject of your adulation is almost always ignorant. They don't know you, have no knowledge of their importance or any idea of how a simple glimpse in a magazine or on TV can spiral in to a cardiac arrest. A crush can feel so profound.

With the advent of music videos, downloadable content, streaming services and TikTok, the preteen has never had more access to the object of their desire or to find an object to desire. It isn't quite the same as it was for me and my friends. For us it was the rock bands of the sixties and seventies who were only too aware of the impact their music, style and looks had on groupies who followed them, sometimes to the death. Bands such as the Rolling Stones, Cream, Led Zeppelin were often surrounded by beautiful young girls, camping outside hotel rooms, jumping fences at concerts, leaping in front of fast-moving vehicles, all committed and compelled to follow their idols to wherever in the world they were playing.

I met my match in my husband. John and I have been together for over forty-five years. This lasting relationship is real, a friendship full of love and children and laughter. But that wonderful feeling, the innocence and excitement of the crush is not present. How can it be? What we have is bona fide, not a trifling thing, but something to cherish and work at to maintain. Crushes aren't like that. The recipient has no input. No respect is received or given. Yet they felt important. Perhaps giving me a head start in knowing true love when it came knocking for the first time.

And now, can I still feel it, the attraction of a good-looking Loki or Legolas? Of course I can, I'm not dead!

Sea States

Jo Cross

THE OFFING

There is a life in which I live close to the sea, close enough to catch the taste of salt on the air, to hear the mewing of the gulls and the susurrus of the swell as it strokes the shingle shore, back and forth, back and forth. If I walk for twenty minutes downhill, I will come to the sheltered bay of a small harbour, a perfect horseshoe gouged out of the cliff-face where river meets sea. There, as always, I will stand and scan the curve of moored boats, listening to the synchronous slapping of halyards on masts, blinking against the shimmer of the early morning sun, my eyes resting, with relief, on that familiar shape — the sleek lines, the cheerful porthole eyes, and the long bowsprit of a Cornish Shrimper.

There is a life in which I head down towards the pontoon, taut with anticipation for the day ahead and all it might hold. The fibre-glass dinghy rocks excitedly as I step aboard, but I settle myself onto the planked seat, release the painter and push off with an oar. Back to the bow, I row, pulling hard, the plash of the oars on the water breaking through the utter stillness of the morning. At first, it seems I am making little headway, but I keep pulling — a steady rhythmic motion. A glance over my shoulder and the Shrimper suddenly looms up ahead of me.

There is a life in which I propel the dinghy around the stern of this small boat and clamber aboard. I greet her like the good friend she is — removing her covers, checking her over, tending to her needs, inhaling her damp, briny smell. Hauling up the nut-brown mainsail, I take the tiller in my hand and, silently, conspiratorially, we leave the mooring and the bay and the awakening land behind us, and head out towards the horizon.

There is a life in which all this is true. But it is not my life.

SEABORNE

I have a photograph — creased, black and white fading to grey. A dark-haired child, barely a year old, dressed in a fussy, ruched bathing costume, is strapped into a rocker in the cockpit of a small sailboat. She has a thumb stuffed into her mouth and looks a little wistful, if one-year olds can be wistful. This is me, I know. I recognise my baby self from other snapshots of the time. The photograph is the earliest surviving image of me on board a boat. There I sit, absorbing, drinking it in, soaking it up.

The boat was called *Dig This*, and was followed by others: *Gay Dog, Nantucket, Nautipus, Tardis*. They all met certain requirements, each boat representing a stage of my father's life, who'd found a second home on the sea. I became acquainted with most of them, got to feel the way they moved through the water, the cut of their jib. *Nantucket*, however — a beautiful, two-masted, 38' yawl — stole my heart. *Nantucket* infected me, the way a place can creep into your soul and linger.

FORCE 5 FRESH BREEZE

My bare feet pad down the deck. I can feel the sharp heel of the boat and the lay of the boards under my toes.

'Hold on tight,' my mother shouts, yet again. I pretend I haven't heard her, but my hands cling onto the wire railings and I'm inching step by step, fist over fist, towards the bow. If she had her way, my mother would keep me safely by her side in the cockpit. But on board, we toe Dad's line, and he said yes.

When I reach the top, I hunker down into position, legs dangling wildly either side of the bowsprit, nothing but a wire between me and the deep dazzling sea.

We are rollercoasting, sails bloated by the wind, cresting the waves. I can feel us rise, up and up, porpoising, as if to take one great leap skywards and then, whoosh, we plummet down, falling away, and I'm lost in a frothing frenzy of spray. I turn my sea-saturated face heavenwards, lick salt-encrusted lips, wipe strands of wet hair from my eyes and scream into the vortex. I am this, here, now, and I want this forever.

ROUND TURN AND TWO HALF HITCHES

Nantucket slips against the ebbing tide, her engine thrumming rhythmically like a pulse. The yellow buoy of the mooring is fast disappearing behind us as we leave the marina. The long pontoon, which pokes into the river like a finger from a shoreline of foul-stinking, inky-black mud, is soon a distant rubbed-out line.

My father sailed a tight ship, and we all knew our duties. There were many things I could do. I could bring the fenders on board and stow them in the cockpit lockers. I could unfurl the ensign and place it securely into the holder. I could attach the burgee and raise it up to the masthead. I could wind the winches. I could help hoist the mainsail. I could take the helm and steer to a given landmark. But there were many things I could not do. I understood sailing in parts, not as a whole. Quite simply, I could not sail. Still can't. I was only ever a deckhand, never a sailor.

As we motored on through the sheltered waters of the estuary and down into Portsmouth Harbour, I would keep a lookout for familiar landmarks. The immense steel flanks of the destroyers and aircraft carriers, at anchor and at peace, stark and forbidding. The three mighty masts of *HMS Victory* scrawled on the skyline of old Portsmouth Dockyard; a warship of a different era, when sail ruled the seas and battles were won by one-armed, one-eyed seamen. The matchstick armature of the roller coaster at Southsea Funfair. The one-hundred-foot tank of water, used, as my father explained, to train submariners to escape a drowning vessel.

It's still there, decommissioned, masquerading as a Gosport tower block. Gilkicker Point, a vital navigational feature when homeward bound. And Spitbank Fort — built in the late 1800s to repel a French invasion which never quite materialised — a perfectly round island of granite, brick and armoured-plating, then abandoned and semi-derelict, squatting in the mouth of the harbour.

By now, we would have entered the open waters of the Solent, a strait separating the Isle of Wight from the mainland. Once upon a time, many thousands of years ago, it was nothing more than a river valley. On a map, the island looks like it has come unmoored and is drifting steadily away to France. The Solent today is both playground and major waterway, a place where every conceivable kind of pleasure craft crosses paths with tankers, container ships, fishing boats, frigates, and liners. On a fair summer's weekend, it hustles and bustles like a street market.

That moment, as we leave the protection of the harbour, when the wind whips up and the shrouds purr, when the sea agitates and waves make us rock and roll, when my father barks orders at his crew and we haul on ropes and wind the winches and the sails rise up. That moment when my father cuts the engine.

MACKERELING

The line goes taut, tight like the string on a violin, whipping through the air, slicing through the wake that trails behind us. A flash, a glimpse of a silver coin in the sea, flipping and tossing. 'Dad, a fish, I've caught a fish!' I shout, and he laughs and comes to stand beside me, guiding me, as I reel it in, and in, and in.

Poor fish. It jerks and gybes, fights to survive, but with every thrash of its body, the hook digs deeper. Poor fish. Landed, exhausted, the mackerel quivers on the deck, hieroglyphics etched along its back, a twitching, shimmering, iridescent thing of beauty. Now, I want to set it free, to let it slip silently back into the sea, as if this had all been one bad dream.

My brother delivers a hard hit to the head, and the mackerel is dead. The line strains again and again — we have sailed into a shoal. Fish after fish slap onto the deck like big fat raindrops. The boat is sticky with blood and scales.

Later, filleted and pan-fried, with butter and a shake of salt and pepper, we eat the mackerel for supper.

SEAPIECES

The way the water moves around us, slaps and chops as the wind meets the tide, eddies within eddies, waves on waves, restless undulations, at once both slick and viscous, thick as quicksilver, and yet somehow insubstantial — spittles of spindrift scattering, coalescing, evaporating.

The way the land looks from the sea — recognisable, like a memory, but utterly otherwhere. Keen to find our bearings, we search out familiarity — church steeple, cliff top dwelling, copse, cove, castle ruin. With our outliers' off-shore-eye view, we read the coastline like back-to-front writing.

The way we always have Baxter's lobster bisque for our first lunch at sea. The hiss of the gas, the clink of crockery, the sweet fishy tang escaping up from the galley below. Like a vending machine, our meal emerges through the hatch, bowl by steaming bowl of phosphorescent orange soup with our father's special touch — a swirl of cream and sherry. The soup is thick and warm and tastes of the sea.

The way the damp bri-nylon sleeping-bag liner twists around my legs, trapping me within, and I lie grub-like, cocooned in my bunk, listening to the lapping of water on wood, watching the stars glister through the skylight.

The way the digestive biscuits taste faintly of diesel.

The way the weather changes in an instant, a sudden squall darkening the skies and whipping the water into frenetic white horses. We huddle in the cockpit, legs braced against the heel of the boat, riding it out.

The way the see-saw sea-swell shifts my equilibrium, destabilizes my land-legs, so that I'm upping and downing long after landfall, bound still to the rhythm of the ocean.

FOUNDERING

The wind was up. Nantucket was flying. We rode her like a stallion, reins short and tight, goading her onwards.

'Right,' said my father, 'we're going to gybe. Jo, when I say, can you release the jib sheet,' he said, pointing to the starboard-side winch. 'Richard, get ready to wind.'

The calm of the cockpit erupted into a frenzy of activity as my father shouted 'gybe-ho' and spun the wheel, pushing the stern of the boat through the wind. My mother, busying herself below deck, chose this moment to pop her head up through the hatch, just as the boom, a mighty beam of solid Douglas fir, swung across the deck, catching her on the temple with a sickening thud. She let out a howl and fell back down into the cabin. We could hear her sobs.

My poor mother. Aboard was not her natural habitat. She endured it but always craved the stability of *terra firma*. My mother, gregarious and engaging, was a huge presence in my life. On the water, I can barely recall her.

I can still remember my father's face as he stood at the helm, the second before he moved towards her. Concern and compassion, but something else besides — a flicker of irritation, a flash of anger at her folly, at her capacity to scupper his joy.

I think it was then that I first saw the cracks, as if the boom had smashed against the urn of my parents' marriage, fracturing it into many pieces that fell, one by one, until the final inevitable collapse.

By then, my father would already have met Lynda, his second wife-to-be, his soulmate, his First Mate.

HOME PORT

The boatyard was a jumble of boats and trailers, recumbent masts, and upturned dinghies in various states of disrepair and repair. Owned by my cousin Chris, it was a familiar backdrop to our lives during the sailing months — snatched summer weekends beetling down the A32 on a Friday evening, catching the tide back home on Sunday.

In early spring, the yard would be deep in preparation for the season ahead, my father up a ladder in his stranded boat with a paintbrush and pot of varnish. I would often wander through the yard, idly watching the coming and going of boats, crews kitted out in their deck shoes, smocks, and oilskins. Sometimes, I would step into the jangle of the big boatshed, voices hollering to be heard over the din of saws, and hammers, and drills, clangs reverberating off the black corrugated iron walls, a sickly whiff of resin in the air.

One morning, I was hanging about the yard when Chris called me over to the on-site chandlery, a small adjunct to the main office, stuffed full of nautical paraphernalia.

'Do you think you could tidy this up a bit?' said Chris, bearded, with the ruddy face of a man who spent much of his life outdoors. We stood in the middle of the room, silently surveying the mayhem around us, until my cousin, distracted by a customer, wandered off.

At that young age, I had little understanding of the various bits of hardware cluttering those shelves. I was, nevertheless, beguiled. To enter the chandler's realm is to enter a wonderland. Even today, I cannot pass a chandlery without stepping inside, for no other purpose than to savour the trove of gleaming gizmos: the brass cleats and fairleads, the hooks and hinges and stainless-steel shackles and stanchions, their forms and functions evoking the romance of the sea, the otherness of being 'aboard'.

Sailing is awash with terminology; it has its own language that serves to over-inflate the egos of its native speakers, whilst intimidating everybody else. You are in or you are out, a sailor or a landlubber.

In the event, I did a good job. I cleared a path through the reels of rope and chain and squidgy fenders to the laden shelves, where I began to sort and classify, creating small, grouped tableaus according to the size and shape of the objects, as painstakingly as I arranged my collection of trolls in my bedroom back home. A warm glow smouldered in the pit of my stomach, the deep satisfaction of restoring order to chaos.

WAY POINTS

I studied navigation once, as if trying to plot a course to find the sea, which was a very long way off.

I'm an inland islander, a midlander, by default not by design. The compass points of our lives are rarely guided by a wish list; we navigate a passage via a series of random opportunities, not visible on any chart.

I sat of an evening at a sticky school desk, surface scratched and scrawled with the utterances of bored teenagers, equipped with charts, dividers, parallel rule and drawing compass. I learnt about dead reckoning and leeway, Lines of Position and speed made good. I listened to the shipping forecast with attention, but without purpose: Shannon, Rockall, Malin, Hebrides. It was absorbing, but pointless. I got no closer to the sea. My aspirations had been an illusion, like the mirage of a Fata Morgana. Unused, my navigation skills languished. I'd be lost at sea now.

Later, I moved southwest by south to the Malverns, still midland. Sometimes at night, when the town sparkles like a string of fairy lights along the contour of the hills, looking out east over the sweep of the Severn valley, I like to imagine the valley is the ocean, dark and inscrutable — a vast body of water stretching out and beyond to unfamiliar, faraway places.

DOWNHAUL

My father sported a jaunty gap between his two front teeth. Wide enough to fit a couple of half crowns, he would say proudly. His lucky gap, my mother said. And if he did seem to lead a somewhat charmed life — although ever the optimist and schemer, I would say he made his own luck — it finally ran out when his beloved Lynda died far too young at the age of fifty-nine.

My father cared for her devotedly at home. During the long, lonely evenings he spent downstairs in his cavernous farmhouse sitting room, as she lay fading in the bedroom above, he pored over brochures for fancy motor cruisers. He was plotting and planning a future without her. At seventy-three, he knew his sailing days were probably over.

For the three decades of their contented life together, my father and Lynda juggled a life on the sea with the pigs and ducks of a smallholding in Devon. Living the dream. I joined them occasionally, as my all-consuming working life allowed. After Lynda died, I made more of an effort to keep my father company: a hop across from Plymouth to Noss Mayo, a buzz up the River Tamar, or down the coast to Fowey. But my father was a sailor at heart and never took to motor cruising.

For his eightieth birthday, he bought himself a handsome 23' gaff rigged cutter, a shot across the bows of old age. Like a swallow returning to an English summer, he'd made his way back. Just in time. The cancer was probably already creeping with malignant intent through his veins.

BLUE WATER

I have crossed seas. From one side to the other, land to land, from here to there and the nowhere in between. I have risen at the crack of dawn, long passage ahead, destination elsewhere. I have left safe harbours and watched them recede, evanescing like memories, becoming indistinguishable from the thin horizon. I have sailed out of sight of all land, sky meeting sea in every direction, our boat a mere speck on a blank page. I have taken my turn at night watch, autopilot holding our course, travelled the moon path, squeezed between the oily obsidian of the waters beneath and the midnight blue above. I have lain on the deck and looked up at that boundless, star-studded velvet dome, drunk on wonderment. I have felt my body wilt with tiredness, eyelids fighting gravity, desperate to be relieved of my duties, to retreat below and wrestle into my sleeping bag, to surrender to sleep. I have woken to the sound of my father in the saloon, the creak of his shoes, the whine of the kettle, the morning news on the radio, me lingering in my salty bed. I have sailed rolling seas too, stomach lurching with every heave of the boat, muscles taut with the strain of holding back the rising sickness, that malevolent, over-whelming presence. Wasted, wretched, guts spewing into the void, I have sold my soul to the devil for solid ground. And I have cried 'land ahoy', spotted that first smudge of somewhere, a chimera that steadily materialises to become there, the other side, journey's end.

HEAD TO WIND

It isn't so much raining as oozing — a mist hangs in the air and settles in droplets on my hair and eyelashes. By the time I've walked from the car park to the ferry terminal I am sodden.

'One return, please.' The woman punches in the numbers on her keyboard, long turquoise fingernails click-clacking on the keys.

'And when will you be returning?' she asks without looking up.

'Sunday,' I reply, thinking, 'as usual.' Except nothing is quite as usual anymore.

I join the queue down the freezing tunnel to the passenger ferry, a spiteful wind sneaking through the joints of its steel panels. I pull the collar of my coat up and stuff my hands deep into my pockets. Normally, I would ring my father to tell him I was about to board.

Slumping into a hard unforgiving, plastic seat, I peer through the blur of raindrops coursing down the window at the relentless grey of sea and sky. Above me, a screen flashes adverts for island attractions: Monkey Haven, The Garlic Farm, The Needles — absurdly incongruous in this bleak winter season. Finally, we are moving, chugging away from the pontoon, through Southampton Water and on towards the Solent and the Isle of Wight where my father now lives.

As we leave the harbour behind us, the ferry surges forward, hitting the waves with a thud, splats of salty water smacking the windowpane. In between the drenchings, I survey a desolate expanse of water — a seascape of echoes, places of familiarity and memory. Wootton Bridge, where my Canadian cousin taught me to row, patiently intoning 'there's no such thing as can't'. The Hamble and chicken in the basket at the Jolly Sailor. Newtown River with its marshy creeks and secretive tideways, terra incognita for me and my brother to explore *Swallows and Amazons*-style in the dinghy. Buckler's Hard up the Beaulieu River, the last place I sailed to with my father, already in his eighties. The last time I ever sailed.

The ferry slows as we near Cowes. I scan the buildings, searching out the balcony where my father would have stood, waving at the ferry, knowing that I would see him. The apartment lies in darkness. We dock, gather our belongings, and file up the gangway. I swing my bag onto my shoulder and walk through the throng of welcome parties. Too late to visit the hospice tonight. I turn right and trudge towards my father's empty apartment.

IN THE WAKE OF

A small wooden sailboat sits on top of my wardrobe, slumped on its side, aground. The paint on its crimson red hull is chipped and the little triangle of cloth sail is authentically greying, as if salt stained and weathered.

The boat is a remnant of a mobile I gave to my father in his later years, a birthday present for a man who had everything. He certainly had no need for a mobile of multicoloured sailboats, but he hung it from the ceiling of his waterside apartment, nevertheless, where it twirled and rocked in the sea breeze when the large balcony doors were pulled open.

When my father died, there was nothing I especially wanted of his. Our house is small, and his taste was not mine. Objects are the flotsam and jetsam of a life, not the memories. But, holding on to something of his, of him, felt like a requisite gesture of respect, a tribute. In the end, I chose one of his customary black wool sailing caps, complete with grubby sweatband, and the little wooden sailing boat.

Things might have been different. I might have had a boat of my own to sail. But this is how it is.

———

HOMETOWN

BARBARA MCMILLAN

We came filled with optimistic certainty. We were new at big decisions. I was not quite out of my teens and Bob was barely older when we vowed to love each other forever. In our early twenties, still shaking off childhood ourselves, we plunged into parenthood. When our baby was four months old, we needed to leave the university community and get on with growing up. Time to close our eyes and jump.

On paper, the little town ticked all the boxes. At least, we pretended it did. Okay, in hindsight we omitted important criteria from the list. But the basic location was acceptable. Neither of us likes city life; I hate cold weather; it was new for us both, a place with no baggage (specifically, none of his ex-girlfriends, if I'm honest). We would be halfway between our families, close enough for visits, distant enough to limit spontaneity. By far, its most attractive feature was that Bob had a solid job offer that featured a pay cheque and health insurance coverage.

On my personal scale of 'appalling' to 'charming', the town was a solid 'adequate' when we came here in the mid-1980s. The area was viable, growing, poised to blossom, swaggering with a bit of pride in holding its own better than towns of similar size. Three major employers were headquartered in the county, and they were booming. With a population of seven thousand, it could not help being provincial and rural, but it is an easy two-hour drive to cities with entertainment options and better shopping.

The land here is nearly flat, its gentle contours filled with pine tree woods and cotton fields marked off with red-clay farm roads. Just outside the city limits, a smattering of businesses, mobile homes, and an occasional house. The community college across the road from a pasture. Closer to the centre of town, fast food restaurants, grocery stores, banks, a hospital, the police station. The public elementary, middle, junior high, and high school. The K-12 private school. Automobile dealerships. No bars, clubs, or pubs — this county is 'dry'. No legal alcohol sales.

There are, of course, many churches. This is the Bible Belt. The two largest, Southern Baptist and the United Methodist, stand diagonally across the street, keeping watchful eyes on each other. Despite their differences, the congregations share a cemetery. The town's largest African American churches are not in that part of town.

From every direction, all roads lead to the same place. 'The Square' is the heart of town. The post office, some lawyers' and accountants' offices, and a variety of small, glass-fronted retail shops and a restaurant stand shoulder to shoulder facing the town's only meaningful landmark, the Old Courthouse. Built at the turn of the twentieth century, it was outgrown by 1960 and replaced by the nondescript, utilitarian brick box that now houses county government. Within walking distance, a handful of Victorian-era houses stand, lovely but ridiculous, among no-frills neighbourhoods built for working-class families after about 1940.

Our young family came here looking for a place to call home. We were open to relocating if opportunity beckoned, but only during our daughter's pre-school years. We were committed to settling down for the long haul once she reached school age. Neither of us had the luxury of staying put from kindergarten to graduation, so we knew the downside of change. Being the perpetual new kid was brutal on relationships as well as on academics. Permanence, roots, a real hometown — those were the gifts we were determined to give our children.

As novice parents do, we envisioned raising our children in storybook fashion. It would be an American dream set in an amiable, encouraging community of dear, life-long friends spawned by the picket-fenced village that banded together to raise our collective children. The next generation would pine for home, sweet home, and our spacious, immaculate house would draw them with irresistible lure for family gatherings at holidays. This could be that place.

Where was Nostradamus when we needed him? The oracles were silent. The town promised to be a wonderful village in which to raise our family, to stitch our story into the fabric of life here, our chosen hometown. So much for promises.

I was born in Atlanta. I cut my baby teeth on the notion of Southern hospitality, confident that the region below the Mason-Dixon line is uniquely warm and welcoming and friendly and safe. If I forgot to say 'Ma'am' and 'Sir' to an adult, I was admonished for 'being ugly'. In the metropolitan areas with more diverse and mobile inhabitants, the rules are somewhat flexible; in rural areas, they are iron-clad. Different manners equal no manners at all. I think it goes back to the 'poor but proud' sensibilities of defeated Confederates.

Bob and I know the rules, and for natural introverts like us, they are exhausting. Greet everyone, strangers and all, or come off as rude, angry, or clinically depressed. Do not be too direct; it is impolite. Leave time for small talk when running any errand, because getting straight to business is rude. A trip to the grocery store to pick up bread and milk can turn into a full-hour outing with all the obligatory fluff-filled conversations:

'How's your family? Did Susie make it into town?'

We jest that the usual queries are summed up in the phrase, 'How's your Mama and them?'

Joke or not, it is no laughing matter. Formulaic pleasantries are as ubiquitous as cricket chirps:

'Oh, please do come in!' and 'You MUST stay longer!' and 'Come back real soon!'

Lack of fluency in the vernacular of such pseudo-invitations might lead to social suicide. These verbal rituals are not benign. Scratch the veneer, and the sleight of hand is visible. Telegraphing amused, belittling superiority masquerading as a compliment, is an art form:

'Oh, thank you, dear. I am sure you tried your best.'

'My, my! I love your dress! I notice how pretty it is every time you wear it.'

'How brave to let your children run around like that.'

I call such remarks *snubmanship.*

Insults are wrapped in magnolia manners. The uninitiated should not take invitations or compliments at face value. Social ambushes and snarky, sarcastic comments may be imbedded in the pleasantries, barbed hooks in the invitations and compliments. Plausibly deniable rudeness hides under the thinnest veneer. Decoding requires insider knowledge.

Here in the Deep South of the United States, we tend toward tribalism. In small towns, bonds are generational. Masquerading as Southern hospitality, introductory chitchat is a weapon. Responses to conversational-sounding inquiry such as 'Where are you from?', 'What brought you here?', 'Who are your people?', separate the sheep from the goats.

The initial sorting is provisional. Sheep often turn into goats and sometimes a goat can jump the fence. We never managed to clear the barrier. Instead, in naïve, oblivious earnestness, we added padlocks and barbed wire with every passing day.

My late father had been a colleague of a prominent local businessman. We were well-educated professionals. We assumed we were shoo-in, hands-down acceptable. But as natives of Birmingham and

Atlanta with no real ties here, we were suspect. The town's more prominent families are descended from its original landowners, bankers, merchants, and politicians and form a cabal that looks askance at big-city strangers. We were outsiders, maybe even carpet-baggers. Knowing the game would not be enough.

Fundamental obstacles to full acceptance started with ascribed lineage and upbringing. After that, it was like an interactive story with forced choices that direct the plot line: 'Would you rather kiss the toad or fight the troll?' Toad, go to page thirty-five. Troll, go to page fifty-two.

In this town, essential filters are such questions as: 'Which church do you attend?', 'What are your leisure activities (hunt/fish or literature/arts)?', 'What organisations do you support?', and another, more important one: 'Which school will your children attend?'

In the early years, we stayed in the holding pen of the unclassified, designated neither sheep nor goats. Then came our mortal sins. One: We chose to send our children to public school[1] rather than to the area 'segregation Academy', a school which even now is racially homogeneous. We remain fundamentally opposed to everything they stand for. Two: I was invited to join a locally prestigious women's social club. I was flattered, but even if I had wanted to join, our straight-jacket budget could not stretch to make the financial commitment. I was never approached to participate in any other community social organisation. I had no inkling my children, especially my daughter, would be excluded by association. Though we were unaware, it was done, with no possibility of redemption.

---

1. Public schools where I live are state government supported and expense to parents is minimal. Transportation to and from school, as well as meals during school hours, are provided at a minimum. Private schools are run by a variety of entities. Though requirements differ from state to state, the one I live in has no accreditation, licensing, testing, or attendance requirements of any kind for private schools. Student registration must be reported to fulfil the compulsory education requirement for children ages 6-17. Funding comes from multiple sources, including tuition and other fees paid by the families.

Buoyed by soap-bubble expectations, we wanted this to be home. So, we settled in, deliberately suspending disbelief. Like the audience in a movie theatre, we overlooked obvious incongruity to preserve the story. And like a carnivorous pitcher plant, the town drew us in.

Renting our first house was unexpectedly difficult. We found one we liked and thought we could afford. I called the realtor to say we would take it; he acknowledged my intention, then promptly signed another couple, saying he had not heard it from my husband, so he did not know we were committing. Because we did not know anyone else to do business with, we let him show us other houses and settled on one. This time, we made sure he understood, and we rented a fifty-year-old fixer-upper a block from the elementary school.

His misogyny was more than a one-time event. We moved in and I noticed sparks when I flipped a switch to turn on a light. I called to report a problem with the electrical system. The agent responded, speaking slowly as if to a child:

'Do you mean sparks when you stick a plug in the socket? That wouldn't be a problem. Or are you sure you mean behind the switch plate, where you turn the light off and on?'

I was rendered nearly speechless. He checked the report with my husband to verify that an actual fire hazard existed before he would put in a repair order.

Turns out, we even selected the wrong realtor. That might seem obvious, but he was wrong for a non-sexist reason; he did not handle property that would put us near people who could ease our path to acceptability. And that mattered.

Soon after our move, our daughter needed routine well-baby medical care. Though no paediatricians practised in town, both general medical clinics would treat her. I called each office and took the first available appointment. The receptionist registered our arrival time and told us to take a seat, pointing to a waiting area to her right.

It was mid-morning, and we were alone in the room. We sat in a faux-leather-covered chair and looked at a magazine. A small basket of easy to disinfect toys stood nearby for waiting children to borrow. Passing through another waiting area on the way to the exam room, I noticed a woman with two young children sitting in a straight-backed, plastic-seated folding chair. There were no magazines, no toys, and the children entertained themselves by running around squealing, as bored children will.

Finished with the doctor at last, we returned to the reception desk to make our follow up appointment. Both waiting rooms were busier, and I noticed that the occupants in one of the rooms were all white skinned; in the other, they were all black. Perhaps it was a coincidence? There were no 1960s 'Whites Only' signs posted, after all. But when I took my daughter back for her follow-up, I found the waiting rooms again contained people sorted by skin colour. We never entered that building again.

The other medical clinic had only one waiting room; people were asked to sit on one side if they were Dr D's patients, on the other if they were seeing Dr W. Our melanin levels were irrelevant and both sides had decent chairs, as well as playthings and reading material.

I slowly realised the town was soaked with racism, laced with classism. It even inspired a woman born and bred here to write one of America's classic novels of social injustice. She got out as soon as she could and only came back to die. Her novel is timeless and true, written in the spirit of hope that we felt when we first settled here.

This town celebrated its bicentennial just a handful of years ago. For the first fifty years, this place was rough frontier. No Civil War battles were fought here — it was not of sufficient value — but it is also the case that the fight has never ended. Cries of 'States' Rights and Segregation' still echo. No aspect of life is immune.

As newcomers, we were wooed by the Academy people, but its all-white faces and white-washed history were not for us. Supporters denied that racism played any role, claiming that the Academy was academically superior, which was verifiably false, and embracing a new narrative that it was a 'Christian' school, and thus morally superior, which was both inaccurate and offensive. The school was not endorsed by any church and had no faith-based curriculum. And Christ does not condone racism.

It is undisputed that the school was founded in the 1970s to avoid racial integration. Some of the founding fathers and mothers had been die-hard determined not to surrender to the federal government's edict; many believed dire consequences would befall society if dark-skinned and light-skinned children were educated under the same roof. In the mid-1980s, parents clung to the myth that their young received a better-quality education and had more opportunities. They were incredulous that we disagreed.

The truth was much more nuanced. In the nineties, the public high school was in the middle of the pack for the state. While its academics were far from excellent by any objective standards, it was nonetheless demonstrably superior to the private school.[2] As for opportunities, that depends on what is measured.[3] Our yardstick favoured diversity.

At that time, many segregation academies remained in the South. Today, the one in our town is the only one in the state that has never accepted a single African American student. Their propaganda claims that they do not discriminate based on race. However,

---

2. As seen in the record of National Merit Scholarships, average college admissions test scores, or any available objective measure.
3. The public school had better extracurricular options, for example. For young people who would be staying in the area, though, there were some networking advantages to attending the Academy. Certainly, attending an Academy made it easier to be selected to join a high-powered university fraternity or sorority, a head-start into state politics. These rain-maker organisations have historically been bastions of segregation. But that was a subculture that we could not have imagined would ever concern us. If we had known, we would not have condoned it.

what quacks and waddles is probably a duck. As recently as 2021, I heard a family member ask:

'What would happen if we let Black children in here? It might be fine when they are little, but what about when they start wanting to date?' Even a mixed-race child of a second-generation graduate of the school was denied admission.

In a short-sighted, self-sabotaging siege, Academy families starved the public system of resources, leaving an embarrassment of low achievement that has crippled both schools. Among the contributing factors, school funding is based on average daily attendance. Even though the private school does not receive tax funding, its existence, and its growth, costs the public school money. It is hard to fathom what a difference it might have made if the time, effort, and money that has gone to the Academy had been invested in the public school.

So, we watched, helpless, as the public schools deteriorated. When our first child graduated, the decline was already in progress; our younger one barely escaped with his diploma before it collapsed. And despite its resources, the Academy provides a sub-standard education, too, perhaps fearing that students will flee if classes are challenging. Graduates of both schools enrol in classes I teach; I see firsthand what their diplomas are worth.

At any rate, the local weekly newspaper, which has somehow refused to die, published a recent front-page headline announcing that no spectators other than parents of players, cheerleaders, and band members would be allowed in the stadium for the high school football game that week because a shooting occurred at a nearby gas station a few days before. There is no known connection between the shooting and anyone connected to football or to the public school system. This is not the first gun violence in the area, or even at that specific gas station. The superintendent of education has been around a few years, so an administration change does not account for the no-spectators stance.

If the ban had not been announced in the paper, no one would have been likely to notice; no one else attends the games, anyway.

The school suffers from lack of community support, poor parent involvement, funding woes, and has rocketed downward in academic performance with frightening velocity over the past two decades.

Spectators continue to fill the private school's stands. The Academy's tiny marching band celebrates the legacy of the Old South by playing 'I Wish I Was in Dixie' at school sporting events. The crowd cheers the song widely regarded as the 'Confederate National Anthem', Nero's proverbial fiddling while Rome burned. The Old Guard still runs the town, but the racist snake has eaten its own tail.

We were ribbons on a Maypole, intertwining with our children's teachers and coaches and scoutmasters and their families at school functions, church, sports, extracurricular activities, and work. With no kin nearby, it was nice having people we could ask to pitch in transporting children or otherwise to help in a jam. But the pretty pattern was superficial, and the dance was short-lived.

The first day of sixth grade, our daughter's delight was palpable when she bounced through the front door announcing, 'This was the best day ever! Sarah is in all my classes!'

Amanda and Sarah were in the same scout troop and played softball on the same team. On weekends and in summer they were often together riding bikes or planning sleepovers. They had never had school classes together, though. What a joyful start to a new school year.

The next day brought tears. 'Everything is ruined. Sarah found out last night they are leaving.'

Her friend had broken the news that she would be moving to another state in just a few weeks as part of an organisational change in her father's employment. My sad little girl had no idea just how bad this announcement was. It signalled change that would rock the community's foundation. And as the economy unravelled, so did the fragile design we had been weaving.

In a tragic but ironic twist, the foundation laid in the education landscape paved the road to the ruination of the area's economy. Our textile, paper, and transportation industries died because of globalisation and market forces, and community leaders made the area so unattractive it could not recover. With a few rare exceptions, the best and brightest of the town's progeny, regardless of race, have walked away. My children do not live here — that is no surprise — but the other children of this village, fourth and fifth generation sons and daughters, the ones with prominent family connections, are leaving, too, and I don't see them flocking here for holidays. The older generation, the folk who shouldered us aside, are following their children to greener pastures elsewhere. Soon, the proud founders of the Academy will have the place to themselves. I am sure they will rest well in their neat rows side by side in the cemetery across town from the African American dead.

Twenty-first century reality check: Families like mine, educated young professionals with children, do not move here. Upwardly mobile families of colour? Not welcome in the private school. The public school is unimaginably bad — in a most ill-advised strategy, the public-school authorities made fatal errors. They refused to consolidate the shrinking schools to improve efficiency, and they lowered the standards again and again to improve graduation rates at the expense of academic quality, and to reduce parent complaints and criticism. It never occurred to the decision-makers that providing an excellent education could be a winning tactic.

The Academy founders, indeed, everyone here, has paid. The golden future they envisioned for their descendants is, as one might say, 'gone with the wind'. What corporation wanting to be competitive on a global scale would choose to locate in such an environment? They threw away all pretence of social conscience to maintain the *status quo*. And their plan failed, creating a permanently disenfranchised, angry underclass.

Regardless of race or *alma mater*, most successful young people flee this place to make their lives, searching for a different sort of hometown for their children, one with acceptable schools, well-paying jobs, and cultural enrichment opportunities. Rather than a sweet little town, they see this place as too small-minded and provincial to raise their children.

Some who walk away may return some distant day. My colleague made a mid-life return; he finds himself teaching at a school he attended forty years or so ago.

In his words: 'When I was a child, this place was run by an Old Guard, a joyless, brutal cadre who ran absolutely everything. If you were not one of them, you could attend, you could serve, but you could never star. In the school play, you could move sets or hand out programmes, but you could not play a lead. You weren't a cheerleader or the quarterback on the football team. You could be in the band, but not the drum major. Even so, I came back here after a series of job changes, a divorce, because I knew I could walk in and be given a chance. I was from here, and I came home.'

I nodded and said, 'But I'm not.'

In the last two election cycles, candidates for local offices ran with campaigns consisting entirely of 'I was raised here. My parents and grandparents are from here, too. I make no claim to be better qualified than my opponent, but he's not from here, so everyone should vote for me.' And damned if it did not work.

Bob did not stay with the job that brought us here for long — not a good fit — so he found a position with an established attorney and worked there on a salary for a while, but that was not financially feasible in the long run. They decided to part company, and Bob set up his first solo practice. I found out I was expecting our second baby days later. By then, I had started working at a part-time, toe-in-the-door job that quickly led to a better one with a modest but steady pay cheque that would carry us through while the law practice grew. And I carried the family's health insurance.

My self-employed husband and my children relied on my employment for insurance from 1986 on. Fortunately, both Bob and I were healthy. Our daughter had ongoing but minor issues with her tonsils and adenoids until they were removed when she was in second grade. Our son, however, was going to require expensive surgery to correct a non-life-threatening condition when he was older. Once his condition was identified, changing jobs could have jeopardised his coverage. We could not take that chance.

As ridiculous as it sounds, insurance held me hostage. At that time, health insurance in the US was tied to employment and was not automatically portable. When I considered changing jobs, I had to consider the risk of the waiting period that could be imposed for any 'pre-existing condition' such as my son's. While not an issue for my family, people with major health issues risked rejection entirely as 'uninsurable'. The technical term for the resulting dilemma is 'job lock', and it was a serious problem.

Life sped by like a thrill-ride. The pre-school years were over in a flash. The school years brought challenges, but we still tried to love this town in verb-not-noun fashion, to act in its best interest, as we invested in creating a hometown for our children. We volunteered with Scouts and school band, organised a Model United Nations team, coached sports, taught Sunday school, created opportunities.

Our children completed their studies at the public high school with a dazzling array of honours and awards, and both were well-prepared for post-secondary studies. When our son graduated in 2006, our self-imposed commitment came to an end. That August, I was awarded the security of tenure[4] at my job, and I loved what I was doing. The president of the school tapped me as the founding director of the school's honours program. It was a dream come true.

Over the next few years, Bob's practice echoed the area's economic climate; neither was thriving. He applied for salaried jobs

---

4. I live in an 'at will employment' state, meaning that employees and employers can part company without due process. That is, employers can fire without notice for any reason that is not expressly illegal. A strange exception exists for public school teachers. Teachers who get 'tenure' have job security, sometimes so much that educating children is forfeited. It is a job-specific benefit; leaving the College would have forfeited my tenure.

to which he could reasonably commute, with the idea that once he got settled, I would apply for college and mental health jobs and relocate as soon as we could sell our house. No opportunities materialised.

Our parents began to require more of our attention. Bob's father had a variety of chronic health problems that were becoming more serious. My mother was diagnosed with stage IV colon cancer. We dealt with that throughout 2008; at Christmas that year, we learned that Bob's mother had bile duct cancer, which was both rare and aggressive. We started 2010 feeling responsible for all of them. By August that year, they were all gone.

Shell-shocked, we muddled through the next months in an emotional fog. Our children were out of the house. Our son had his surgery. Our parents were dead. Our obligations thus discharged, we could have left. However, we were just exhausted, overwhelmed, undone. So, when the Circuit Judge offered to appoint Bob as Circuit Clerk, we took the path of least resistance and he accepted the position as heaven-sent, with the understanding that he would run for election when the term expired two years later. He did, and he won. We were committed for six more years.

He left elected office and reestablished his private practice. By then, I had been teaching for sixteen years, and I needed a little more time in the system to retire with a reasonable pension.

I have enough time in to retire now. But when we consider leaving, I empathise with my mother's refusal to sell her house. She and my father lived there for ten years; he died in the garage. A decade or so later, it would have been sensible for her to move closer to my sister and me. Inertia trumped reason.

Our discussions of the logistics of relocation start with our boat-anchor of a house. We have just paid off the mortgage. Empty houses are common; it would be a buyers' market if there were any buyers. In the late 1990s when growth plateaued here, it took four years to sell our 'starter' house. The real estate market is slower now. The key to selling a house is location, location, location — and timing.

The effort it would take to clean it and repair it in preparation to sell would be considerable but manageable; the emotional investment of reducing our belongings collected over our forty-plus years of marriage, along with the objects acquired at the deaths of our parents, laden as they are with sentimental value, is Herculean.

We meant to create a stable legacy, a firm foundation. Our determination proved foolhardy, irrelevant to one of our children, burial while alive to the other. One lives abroad, the other 'Up North' in Ohio, a state I had never seen before her move. To my simultaneous sorrow and delight, they are both misfits in the town we find ourselves unable to escape.

For now, the aspirational vision of our progeny visiting our spacious, comfortable house in the country, riding horses, raising chickens, growing a garden, learning to cook and shoot and sew and fish and use hand tools with their instant companions, the offspring of our old friends and neighbours, has crashed headlong into reality. Our house is not spacious, and we do not live far enough in the country for horses or chickens. I have a knack for sending plants to see Jesus, not for gardening, and I don't sew. We have cooked, shot targets with a low-power pellet gun, and Bob has supervised a couple of construction projects, but safety concerns with my neurodivergent grandchildren limit hand tool skills. So much for that, then. And no close friends with children or grandchildren of the right age/sex to be good companions have remained in the area.

Yet our granddaughters love visiting our town. Life for them here is so different than their usual break-neck schedule. The allure may be its primitive, exotic feel, but our egocentric speculation is that they would love wherever we happened to be. Who can know? They both think they want our house when we pass on. We pray that they always remember this place fondly — and that they find the hometowns of their dreams.

NAMESHAPE

ALISON M. TEMPLETON

I f I had been named Gillian or Judith, and lived in the pages of Elinor M. Brent-Dyer's *The Chalet School* books, then perhaps my socks would have been whiter, my hair wouldn't have tangled, and I would have been prettier and cleverer. I wasn't, though. Alison Mary it was. Alison, with that boy bit at the end. And Mary? That was okay as it was Mum's name and Jesus' mum's name, though rather old fashioned and boring.

If I didn't fit my name, then who was I? When the auctioneer had slammed his hammer down, the boxes had been packed and the Land Rover traded for a car, somehow Alison Mary went missing. Everyone thought I was there, with them, but I wasn't. I was lost. So, perhaps, if I could be some other girl, I could be found, and then the new, frightening world in which I found myself would be more bearable.

Not so many years before, my name had sat comfortably in the primary school register and proudly on the bottom of the picture I painted of a shipwreck and excitedly sent in to a Blue Peter competition, that famed BBC TV children's programme.

Yes, it was useful to have this name. It told me apart from the other children. It was my name for other people to use. But my name, inside me, was so very much longer, and never written down because it came about before spelling was much of a thing for me. Inside was who I really was, and that was different. Different from the outside name that people called me.

It happened like this, this name of mine inside me, that was me. It happened on the farm where I was born. Names were shapes and colours, sounds and smells, textures and tastes, long before they were letters making words on a page. They were all around me, outside, indoors, wherever I went. I was made up of these. All woven together.

One of the earliest names I learned was Neapolitan. This was the name of my summer cotton dress, blocks of pastel shades, aligned side by side in vanilla, strawberry, mint and chocolate. I look at the only memorabilia I have of this dress, a black and white print of me wearing it, aged three. Yet here, in this monochrome, I know myself ice cream flavoured.

Another was Tortoiseshell Cat, splodged black, tan and white in a random glossy coat. She imprinted herself on me. Tortoiseshell Cat was allowed in the house. Tortoiseshell was privileged among the feral farm cats. They killed rats and mice, I was told, so we wanted them to stay and gave them a daily feeding of the scrapings from the breakfast porridge pan. All the other cats were nameless and formless, indistinguishable. I saw them, a living, moving mass around that porridge dish, then creeping away, disappearing into hidden hunting grounds of sheds and barns and haystacks. Tortoise-shell was soft and familiar. The rest were darkly mysterious secrets. I was deeply wary of them.

As spring warmed us up, the insides of my bedroom window were less often glazed over with wondrous icy formations. Now the winter-soggy Kent Wealden clay pastures gifted frothing flowery blobs of the palest lilac. Milk Maids, we called them. Here our brown and white Ayrshire cows grazed, and in the milking parlour the milk streamed into sparkling glass jars, to a rhythmic pumping sound. Then onwards it went, into the vast vat of collective silky whiteness in the dairy, and on again, into the daily milk tanker and away down the track. But our milk arrived in the kitchen each morning, in great white china jugs of varying sizes, unpasteurised.

And there was one particular name, shaped so large I couldn't take in its form – the green pasture called Leg of Mutton. That name sound lodged inside me, with no questioning of its meaning, no comprehension that my bottle-fed orphan lambs were obliquely related to it. Such delicious warmth of lamb and bottle; the grip I needed to prevent the bottle being wrenched from my hands by the strength of suck and pull; the milky dribble and woolly depth; the pink-tongued, pitiful, incessant bleat when the bottle was drained empty; and the smell and skin-soft sensation of lanolin. I was as much lamb as they.

The umbilical cord of farm was cut when I was nine. We moved away. I unravelled. I was no longer Alison Mary Templeton, Neapolitan-flavoured, Tortoiseshell-coloured, Milk Maid frothing, lanolin lamb milk-dribbled. Nor was I Mr Tickle's sweet shop-treated (yes, truly, the village sweet shop was run by Mr Tickle), or primary school paddock PE-lessoned.

I was no more the snowdrops by the pond, the farm boundary river where our Golden Retriever swam, or our straw bale houses, or thrown around in the back of the Land Rover with no suspension. No more was I tea under the white lilac tree, or the paper chains at Christmas hanging from the oak beams, for that is what oak beams are for. I wasn't, anymore.

Where did that early childhood deep-self knowing and belonging go? That elemental identity of unfettered being. From all that defined me to a barely knowing or being known. To an existence of bewilderment, dislocation, fear, absorbing, discovering, experimenting, failing, finding. And sometimes thriving. The journey was long. Is long. For it takes a lifetime back to unfettered.

My own name, the one I was called, that I spelled out and wrote down, no longer fitted. This name of mine that I have long since understood to be my parents' deliberate choice to anchor me to paternal Scottish blood and to my mother. To origins and values. To my belonging.

But back then, all those years ago, I belonged to a farm, as near to me as breathing. Where I grazed and grew beside the lambs and calves, where I flowered beside the Lily of the Valley, the Pussy Willow and the Bluebells. Where I too fruited in the Quince grove, beneath the Damson and Plum rows, along the hedgerow Blackberries and Hazelnuts and sang along with the Blackbird and Robin. My DNA and theirs, hooked and entwined, as if it were a mycorrhizal fungi community, co-dependent, indistinguishable. That was my name.

If I could have taken this little child of me in an embrace, hugged her tight and held my heavy head against her small one, my white gold hair flopping onto her conker bronzed crown, I could have told her. That it will somehow, eventually, all be alright. But as it is, with the way of children, instead she shows me. Just as organic matter breaks down in the soil, the trauma and loss of farm-being would gradually decompose. In time, nutrients would be released and new growth come.

There would be a flourishing again. The DNA life force of soil, soul and generations would straggle and strand and shape her onwards. This seedling child of me would turn sapling-sized, and one day, in times to come, would look down from the branches of her wide and outstretched arms to teeming life within and around once more.

Spelling didn't come that easily to my little self. When I laid claim to the family set of Beatrix Potter books and wrote my name in the front of each, I was Templton. The up and down letters were definitive, exciting! It was the overall shape that mattered, not the middle. Pushing up the nib of the blue fountain pen, marking a tall thin trail of wet shiny ink on the page. And down, down below the line, for the *p*, a loner down there. It was shape that mattered.

Grandpa Templeton embodied the shape of our name, his name. Everything about Grandpa Templeton was long and tall and straight and narrow and up and down, never across and sideways. Legs were long, arms were long. Invariably his trousers were a bit too short because he was a bit too long. It was a long way down for him and when his ageing legs didn't bend very well, a little help to sit was welcome.

Grandpa had a shooting stick, stainless steel, Featherwate, described on Etsy today as 1950s Country Gentleman, vintage. Grandpa to a T: a folding T, to unfold and sit on, and a pole poking down, with a spike on the end, to secure into the ground. This Featherwate resides now, along with umbrellas and walking sticks, in a holder by my front door. Grandpa died when I was fifteen. No doubt his coffin was long, but what I remember most of his funeral day was Granny, curled and smaller than before.

All the Templeton men, my brother and way back through each generation to at least Great Great Grandpa, were tall and thin. I didn't inherit the height, but did do well with some of the length. I was told my arms were long (I was quite proud of that) and invariably sleeves of school blouses and blazers were short on me. When Mum knitted my cardigans and jumpers she added extra rows to the sleeves.

Templeton, formed with those strident ascender and descender letters, Grandpa both embodied and lived out the shape. He struck out, up and down in his life. His father, Great Grandfather, moved down South as far as he could go, from Ayrshire to Kent, to start his own farming life. Here, in the early years of the twentieth century, Grandpa forged out and upwards and was one of the first to gain a B.Sc. in Agriculture, newly recognised as an academic degree. Immediately afterwards he chose to volunteer, before conscription, in the London Scottish Regiment, to serve in the First World War.

Then down he went to the desert sands, serving most of his war in Palestine ('The oranges there were the best I've tasted in my whole life'), and on and up through the ranks to Captain. After the war he was one of the first lecturers and college principals to teach women agriculture and land-based studies. A pioneer, he paved the way for me. Never forgetting Scotland, homeland of his fathers, he sought and married his bride there.

Templeton flows from my pen, soil darkens my fingers and clogs my boots, and the wind whips and tangles my hair. There's a yearning in me. I find myself looking up, down and around for Templeton all over the place; on war memorials and gravestones, in bibliographies, film credits, bookshops, in places where I have no known connections. On road signs.

In Devon there is a hamlet named Templeton, signposted from the North Devon link road. Obviously, I had to turn off to find it. I flew into Vancouver and took the metro into the city and was startled, no elated, to find we stopped at a station called Templeton. Later I found a Vancouver diner, The Templeton ('Quality Food, Snappy Service'). There are Templetons to find and meet; known of, but as yet unmet relatives, and many others who probably aren't. I'm looking. Looking for connections, for threads and strands, nutrients I'm hungry for, growth. I haven't had enough Templeton. Enough adventures, discoveries, learning, rising to the challenge. And not nearly enough Alba (Scottish Gaelic for Scotland). It is as though Grandpa is leading me by the hand, and we haven't got there yet.

Where is there? Sometimes I don't want to venture anywhere at all. Home is nourishment and contentment. It's a comfy, rounded place, Owen shaped, the shape of my maternal family.

I learned to spell out Owen for Grandma Owen and for aunties and uncles and cousins, on envelopes for cards and thank you letters. I liked the big O. It took a lot of care to write it so the start and finish joined up in a big round circle. Yes, O was a good letter to have. There's a rhyming to my first and last names because of the *o*. Owen, with that big O, makes me feel warm and snug.

Traditionally, Owens didn't travel far – a bit of zig zagging of the generations around East Kent, and a total of perhaps sixty miles between any particular place of birth and death. And Owens were quiet people. It's a common misunderstanding that quiet people don't have much to say, erroneous to think there isn't a lot going on inside. True, it might feel harder to get to know a quiet person initially, but the discerning would hear an Owen speak from their conduct more than their spoken word. Me, my brother and my cousins, Grandma's nine grandchildren, sat in school uniform photos on her shelf. No ranking there, of age or beauty or achievement. Love doesn't get ranked.

I can't remember Grandma Owen's voice, to hear her spoken word. That's another layer of loss, to realise one can no longer hear a loved one's voice in memory. I can remember Grandma's physical presence very well though. There were no straight or sharp edges to her. So many roundnesses without, and within. A gentle, smiling face and kind eyes, hair in one thick grey plait wound up into a bun, pinned in place. It was a terrible shock when I once stayed with her, and my first sighting in the morning was of her in her dressing gown, long plait hanging down her back. That wasn't my true Grandma. My Grandma's hair was round!

Grandma was steak and kidney pudding in a round white china pudding bowl. She was bread and butter and a round bread board with almost my own name on it. This Allinson's Flour bread board is worn now, the letters wearing away, becoming indistinguishable, scored across. I take this bond that is Grandma and me down from the shelf most days at breakfast time. We are beech, I think, turned, not sawn, to create our shape. I don't have to go searching for Owens. They are there, always present, quiet, rounded, warm, homely. They didn't go far and nor do I need to. I don't yearn for more Owen. I have a full helping already.

A partnership nomenclature of my two family names and two long-gone, beloved Grandparents. 'Templeton' with its strident ascenders and descenders, going places, here, there; 'Owen', that rounded, solid base always to bring me home. Mostly they reside harmoniously within me. Sometimes Grandpa's pull to go, do, requires too much of me, so I sit with Grandma by her coal fire. At others I am restless, and Grandma will slowly rise and hold the door open for me so I can go out into the world to play. The door stays wide open for my return and Grandpa can't wait to hear of my adventures. It's a pretty perfect partnership, my two family name shapes.

'It's the jizz.'

'What do you mean, "jizz"?'

I am a young adult, a fledgling birdwatcher, with my new, first pair of binoculars and an experienced friend.

'It's the word for how the bird looks overall, its shape and behaviour. Where it is, what it's doing. If you get a good look, you can see colour and maybe hear its voice too. But first and foremost, it's shape and behaviour. And habitat as well of course. We call it the jizz of a bird.'

I soon realise there's jizz about different types of birdwatchers too. Some are hell-bent on maximising their sightings and making lists and careering all over the place for the rare and spectacular. Some, mainly men, have huge telescopic lens cameras; a jizz of optics and man in one creature.

I baulk if anyone suggests I'm becoming a 'twitcher'. I never check-list or career around. I do freeze on the North Norfolk coast looking at over-wintering ducks, geese and waders. I dawn chorus in May at unearthly hours. I watch and wait, wired with anticipation, beside a Scottish Highlands loch for the osprey to dive into glassy stillness and rise with a fish dangling from its talons.

Back home, I marvel at the immaculate, life-size paintings in the Ninth Reprint 1965 edition of *The Observer's Book of Birds' Eggs*, an artist's brush attempt to show the utter perfection of form and colour. I see how the Kingfisher pours all its palette into its plumage of fire-cracker orange and electric blue, leaving its egg pure white, while the Blackbird saves its artistry for its egg of pale greenish blue with fine, reddish-brown, randomly-flicked speckles. I grieve that

Grandpa's *Readers Digest AA Book of British Birds 1972* talks of common birds which certainly aren't. How can it possibly be that our dear, familiar House Sparrow has declined by seventy percent since publication? Did we simply take it for granted?

I wonder if I too have my own jizz. At one time I seemed to receive gifts of all sorts of 'Alison' paraphernalia — mugs and coasters and fridge magnets, tat really, each depicting a dodgy dictionary of 'Alison' meanings. They variously told me I was noble, truthful, dainty, pretty, loving, imaginative, fun to be with. In appearance and behaviour, I sought to believe at least some of this to be true of me.

I lose myself in marshes, woodlands, mudflats, river valleys, glens, cliff tops and seascapes. And my garden. All this time I absorb the jizz and often give up on identifying (Waders and Warblers — so challenging!) because, after all, a name is just a name. I try to learn birdsong, with limited success. I'm more of a visual person; see that flight, movement, colour, courtship, the way it feeds and how near it dares to approach when I am still and silent!

There are 70,000 known native species of birds, animals, insects and plants in the UK. That makes for an awful lot of jizzes. Naming things clearly does help. Writer and naturalist Mark Cocker in *Claxton: Field Notes from a Small Planet*, a diary of notes from his home village in Norfolk, says of the names of our native species 'Each of them... is an open-ended proclamation about the possibility of a closer relationship. A name is an invitation to intimacy and even friendship... allowing human observers to claim that living creature as part of their own experience.'

I claim, through the bird colour spectrum, Goldcrest, Greenfinch, Blackcap. I make for my own the behavioural names of the Dipper, Shoveler, and Woodpecker. And shape too: Crossbill, Tufted Duck, Crested Tit. And in friendship and intimacy, one of my favourites — the Long-tailed Tit, those miniature fluffy blobs with fine, slender, elongated tails and a voice as tiny and restless as they.

But this naming thing is not always quite that straightforward.

Names can easily elude the pinning down of exactly which creature. Grey and Yellow Wagtails both have lots of grey and yellow feathers, so which is which? They never stand side by side for comparison. Long and Short-eared Owls are so called because of tufts of feathers, not ears, and these aren't related in any way to the birds' hearing. No, for relationship with a wild thing there must be more, so much more, than purely its name.

I met my first Long-eared Owl when walking on the Balmoral estate in Scotland's Deeside on a grey, high summer afternoon. A congregation of little birds were twittering in Silver Birch scrub down below me, on the side of the loch. I stopped, looked, listened — high-pitched, fast twittering, so something was up.

Before I could lift my binoculars, I spied a large, dark blob in one of those Silver Birch trees, at head height. I focussed. I was face to face, eye to eye, with a Long-eared Owl. No wonder all that consternation from the potential prey of this fierce-looking hunter. True to the misnomer, on the top of its head tall, erect tufts, not ears, pointed skywards. Brilliant, rusty orange eyes, with pitch-black pupils, were set in the classic owl-rounded facial disc of tiny pale ochre feathers. Those staring eyes, staring at me. The little birds were safe now. I was the object.

I was mesmerised. To be held in the gaze of a wild thing is nigh on the ultimate gift. I was lost in its shape, plumage, its stance, its eyes. From that slender tree we met. The minutes passed and the world was Owl and me. More minutes. And more. As I slowly rose from some deep, elemental place within, I wondered which of us would break the stare. Owl or me. The sky was darkening, and drizzle started. I had some miles yet to go so I didn't want to get soaked. Still no shifting of Owl, body or eyes. I opened my rucksack and pulled out my over-trousers. Noise and movement. The Owl was still. I put them on. Still stillness. I secured my rucksack as the rain came. More stillness. We resumed our encounter. Rain dripped from my waterproofs and droplets slid down the Owl's feathers. And then, without fuss, I was dismissed. It closed its eyes. I could go.

For those minutes Owl and I had breathed the same air, heard the same sounds, inhabited that remote landscape together. I went. Owl stayed. It was Owl and I was me and we had met and shared a splice of our lives together. I was far from home yet perfectly, wonderfully, extraordinarily at home, with a story to tell on my return. The door would be open, the fire lit and my adventures eagerly shared.

Home. When I stopped mowing my back lawn Common Dog-Violets came. They were there all the time of course; tiny, rounded, heart-shaped leaves deep in the sward. But I, erroneously, had cut them off, regularly, as all good, tidy gardeners were taught in past eras, so they didn't get the chance to flower and seed and spread. I've now freed them from their imprisonment. And Milk Maids! Oh, the joy of just a couple of stems, initially, of Milk Maids! They too seed and have spread a little but it's probably a bit too dry for them — it's not the clay of the farm here in my quarter acre. Its other names are Lady's Smock and Cuckoo Flower, the latter because it flowers when the migrant Cuckoo returns here to breed from over wintering in Africa. I don't hear the Cuckoo. I can't remember the last time I heard the Cuckoo here.

I've used no pesticides or herbicides for years. I don't 'weed'. I only remove plants, be they native or ornamental, when they end up in the wrong place or I don't want them to spread. Wild flowers mingle in with the ornamentals. The insect life has exploded since the mowing stopped. Creeping, crawling, buzzing, weaving, munching, mating, burrowing. Little ant hills have started to build up. Ant hills are a sign of old meadows. I'm creating old meadows!

In late July each year a friend scythes the wildflower lawns. The swish, the arc and accuracy, it's mesmerising. It's a scented soul-massage. I rake into rows, turning them for a week or so and see the green fade into blue-grey hues and gentle buffs. Once dried, I stuff into used compost bags and leave by the roadside — 'FREE Organic hay from my wildflower lawns.' It all goes and feeds or beds pets somewhere or other. Most of all I hope it prompts others to do the same with their lawns.

I'm learning about my mammals too. I borrowed a bat detector — Serotines and Pipistrelles and Noctules. Once, a long time ago now, I saw a Stoat dart across the path and again once, only once, I saw a Hedgehog. Badgers come regularly. They love to scrump and munch up sweet, fallen James Grieve apples and over-ripe dropped Damsons. But they won't touch the fallen Bramleys — too sour, I guess. Blackbirds, and if the weather is mild, Red Admiral butterflies, feed on these well into winter.

'You've created a whole ecosystem here.'

A friend sits in the garden and gazes around, beyond the tray of teapot and milk jug, china and cakes. She gets it. That I have to live and breathe the natural world, be it far flung, or here at home where I am, farmer no, but land manager, conservationist, gardener. We talk of a mutual friend and her pristine, ordered, precise garden, a straight-jacketed space of ornamental expectation which demands too much of my attention, where I'm unable to simply be me.

I sit in my striped deck chair in my lower garden where there's sunshine and dappled shade. It's a woodland edge type habitat. I'm leaning back a little, as deck chairs want you to, binoculars in my lap, and gazing up at the trees and the sky and the clouds, feeling the warmth of the sun. I'm not looking at or for anything much, just being here. A pair of Speckled Wood butterflies flit and dance together. Dark brown ground colour of the wings and yellow-buff spots, in and around sunny woodland glades and rides. Speckled Wood. A name offering friendship, intimacy.

The pair cavort nearer and nearer through the warm sunlit air. I am still and silent, merging into the deck chair beneath me, only moving my eyes to follow them. No more than eighteen inches from my face they pass, and I feel the breath of their wingbeats brush my skin.

I took root and grew, in soil, soul and DNA, in two formative habitats. At the farm, in all its abundance and benevolence; and within my primary school playground. Alison Mary Templeton sat scripted in blue fountain pen ink in the school register of ninety or so village children. There, out in the playground, red and white gingham check, Clarks sandals, white ankle socks, hopscotch, and a skipping rope. And Ivy-leaved Toadflax.

This tiny plant clung to the school playground walls and mattered. She mattered as much to me as my rounded, motherly teacher and my best friend. They both left my life when we left the farm, but Ivy Leaved Toadflax stayed. She's clung to me ever since. Her stems creep and trail, reaching and stretching out, rooting as they go. She drinks and feeds from the scantiest means. Her shiny leaves are bright evergreen and rounded, lobed, a little like ivy, and her flowers are dainty and lilac, miniature Snapdragons.

She attached her name to me long before I could write her down. She was fairy tale. There was something magical about her. Those little lilac faces, the colour of Parma violet sweets, with a brush of egg yolk yellow, she smiled at me from her inhospitable home on the Victorian stone walls which kept in the tarmac and the children.

She inhabits the old places: churchyards and cemeteries, between flagstones and within crumbling pavements and walls.

She clings, to foregone, bygone, long-gone attachments, and makes anew in barren, oft-abandoned dwellings.

She fits in the cracks in broken places. In spite of it all, she makes her belonging.

And so must I.

WHERE THE MAGNOLIA BLOOMS...

MANA JAY

I have been here before.
Trod this stretch of stone and sodden earth,
Turned into the sting of a passing spritz,
Melted into the warmth of your embrace.

I was no stranger to moving cities, yet the move to London was the only one of my own making. Almost. I chose the man, not the place. It wasn't planned. It was quick. I caught myself off guard as much as I did anyone who knew me at the time. Bright red car with an ailing engine. Maybe it was exhaustion, one last sputter. Or, an act of rebellion. Mostly, I think it was serendipity. From December 2008 to the following April, I turned off the ignition. No maps, no steering, no speed controls. I rolled with the road and that road led here.

Fifteen years on, all roads still lead here.

Escape. Hidden deeds unseen. Unspoken words unheard. Friends and family everywhere. I grew up with too much and not enough. I grew up with an itch just under my skin. An itch that itched more when I scratched. I grew up wanting to moult.

Control. I was sexually abused by a distant relative at the age of seven. I wouldn't have known it at the time, but that is when the seed of being rudderless was planted. Nourished by self-blame and loathing, it germinated, took root. Tendrils spread like swallow-wort vines thwarting all that was green. Turned to ED, an eating disorder. She tamed the invasive cirri... and me.

Invisible. *'You look ill.'* I was. *'Being this skinny doesn't look nice.'* I knew. *'A little flesh on your bones is attractive.'* I wasn't. *'Why won't you listen?'* I would if I could.

Yearning. *'Papa's getting transferred.'* I had stopped asking where. New places, new faces and me... the outsider everywhere.

Then I fell in love. He was going to be my great escape. The one to right all wrongs. I was finally going to belong.

Funny isn't it, how we expect so much of just one. It's not ingrained. A mother is a mother, a father a father, a brother a brother, a sister a sister... each one with a singular role. Yet the one I chose to share my life with, I needed it all and more from him.

'You are too proud.' *Crack.*

'You live in a bubble where everything is perfect.'

Perfect? *Crack, Crack.*

'It's always your way or the highway.'

It didn't feel like life was going my way. Maybe it wasn't going his way either.

I was 28 when the illusion dissolved. He was failing to be who I needed him to be. Perhaps, no I am sure, I was failing him too.

It was no wonder that our fledgling union faltered. Weighed down by expectations, his and mine. Two sets of unrealisms perched atop virgin wings that folded before they could spread. I remember the moment, hot and white. Chest rising and falling without effect. Blood running amok. The beat of it echoing in my ears. Nauseous. Lightheaded. Dissociating from a life that was meant to be mine. Again.

Fog of disillusionment. Resentment curdling the air. All I wanted was to flee. And so, I did. Out of the flat, out of the building, away from the compound, away from the tauntingly lush avenue, away from the mess of my shattered stupidity. Marriage wasn't the abracadabra I had hoped for.

I walked till my pulse wasn't pounding, till the knots in my chest weren't quite as tight. I walked till my lungs started working, the world no longer white. Breathe in, breathe out, repeat. It could have been three minutes, thirty or warped a few centuries back in time.

That's where the street I found myself on belonged. Spillage of the Georgian era. Symmetrical townhouses. Sky flaring at the end of the row, showcasing the steeple of a church rising heavenward. An arrow of trees down the centre of the road, funnelling toward the church, marking the way to its blood-red door. I would have felt compelled to explore had my feet not turned right on instinct.

A tiny plot littered with headstones presided over by a single tree. Branches open, bursting with goblet blossoms exhaling creamy pinkness with every breath. A moment you read about in books or watch in films, not one to interrupt an already cinematic panic attack. Yet there I was, powerless against the pull of a modest burial ground and the magnolia that marked its heart.

I have been here before.
Only I haven't.
Not in this body.
Not in this life.
Not in this time.

I soon discovered I had not walked far at all, simply chanced upon Church Row ('show piece of Hampstead' according to Mavis Norris), St John-at-Hampstead and its additional burial ground. A place I would return to again and again.

I was 28 when the itching abated.

It became my place, my elixir.

A tingle, a prickle, a stirring of the fine hair at my nape; whenever I was discomposed, I would find my way there. Sometimes the plain, black gate stood ajar, sometimes I had to squeak my way in. Some days, the grass was verdant and welcoming; on others, thick with nettles, wild and armed to defend.

At times, it was impossible to reach my magnolia, at others, a carpet of ochre paved the way. I would pick a path through the headstones, careful not to step heavy onto hallowed ground. We had become acquainted and were friends now, me and all of those who were laid there. To most, the tree was prettiest a-blush, to me she was just as vivid bare. Is it her or the spot she marks? The serenity that surrounds her settles my hackles regardless of what she wears.

I was 28, 29, 30... I am 44. Her outstretched arms still welcome me home.

To ache for something,
To see, feel, hear, taste,
To hold it,
Only to ache for it ever more.

It wasn't instantly welcome, this sensation that felt like belonging. Much desired, but not easily acknowledged.

'It doesn't matter where we live, wherever your father is, is home.' I grew up hearing my mother say these words. She hasn't for a while. Not since 2021. My father passed away that year.

'It doesn't matter where we are, as long as my husband is there, it's home.' My sister-in-law's voice lingers in my ear.

'I can travel to the most picturesque of places, live in the most exotic hotels, but nothing compares to home.' My aunt on her two-bedroom flat which she prefers to live in over her rather large house in the same city.

I wasn't meant to feel like this, not here. And yet a sense of safety flowered, the security of coming home, not to a person, not to bricks and mortar, but to this place in Hampstead. It would be years before I learned that Hampstead evolved from Hām-stede, Anglo-Saxon for homestead.

'How are you settling in?'

'Alright, I miss home.' A lie.

I didn't speak my truth to my family, for if I did, what would I say? Was my reaction to this spot, my instant attachment explained away as déjà vu, a glitch in my neuronal matrix? But déjà vu does not occur so consistently, and, if it did, I had bigger problems than the conundrums of place.

'My first trip to Cornwall, it all seemed so surreal. I knew I had lived a life there before this one. I stood on a cliff and saw it unfold,'

my gorgeously lissom, tarot-reading, in-touch-with-her-spiritual-side cousin shared. I hadn't said it before, but I did to her; replace Cornwall with Hampstead, the cliff with a hill and it was exactly the way I felt.

———

'Reincarnation is a process of moving from one stage of mind to another. Whether you are in a body or out of a body is immaterial.'
Frederick Lindemann (at least that's what Google says).

'What did I do in my last life to deserve this?' Universal lament when things go awry. I would be lying if I said I hadn't lamented myself this way.

'You are carrying the burdens of a past life.' Explanation for bad things happening to good people. I had found comfort in it as well.

'In my next life I want to be a dog, a dog like Pepper, in N's house.' Common response to the lavish lifestyle of my parent's Doberman Pinscher. The Doberman has now been replaced by my mother's Shih Tzu, even more pampered than her predecessor. The uncomplicated life of overindulged pets seems most appealing some days.

'I don't want to carry this bad karma into my next life.' Reminder to make good choices in the face of morally difficult decisions. The thought crosses my mind whenever in a bind.

'It will be better in the next life.' Hope that carries you through rough times. Tomorrows are for a reason, it is said. For Hindus, that tomorrow is another life. Classrooms in the school of our soul, graduating from one to the next, and when the soul has learned all it can, nirvana.

I grew up surrounded by echoes of reincarnation. Prepped and primed as I was, I found it hard to believe. My fractured faith (Hindu by birth, agnostic in life) and scientific scepticism stood in the way.

London, 2022

'You will feel like you are watching a movie.'

'Relax. Focus on the crystal on your forehead. Let your mind drift away.' And it did...

Stuck in liquid tar. Limbs congealed, a sticky mess. Duelling darkness. Twisting, turning, billowing black, contortions, merging folds.

A chink in the armour, a bullet hole. A shaft of light, two, three... chomping up the tenebrosity, stygian wisps remain. Stubbornly they pirouette, twirl in liquid gold. Eyes drink in the ombré; emerald, peacock, purple disappearing into grey.

Then I feel the physical, breathing, burgeoning pain. On the horizon a silhouette, one and many more. Voluminous, heavy fabric catching on tall blades. A split in the sky, a prick on my skin, a squelch in my toes, it's cold.

Scorching in my belly, unconscious, then awake. Monastic garb, firm hold on arms, descending vermilion veil. Whispered words, 'Let go child' feathered in the wind.

Warmth butterflying down my back, I bend and kiss a mound. Salt of earth sticks to my lips, a tear, another stain the ground. Stone of cross I hold on to, as the vision begins to fade. Bark of tree I press into, as I let it slip away. Energy of Sol comes flooding, 'You are here, for her...' rippling the tide. Aureate waves recede into hazel-grey eyes.

...with that I come to.

'When you go deep enough, you feel everything.' I did.

'Recall is sometimes painful, accompanied by tears and fears.' It was.

My tryst with past life regression was sensory, physical. I emerged spent, not remembering why I had experimented in the first place. Research is the reason I would give people; trying to find a connection to this place is what I would tell myself. Perhaps I was trying to discredit the latter and find an attachment instead, to the land of my DNA, where I was meant to belong.

My father had passed away a year before. I hadn't grieved for him yet. For if I did, it would mean he was truly gone. I was forced to let go of his corporeal form; I wasn't ready to let go of more. Maybe I could be a Hindu in part and believe that his spirit was still here, lounging in a space somewhere, waiting to be reborn. *'Souls travel together,'* another echo, maybe we will be together again. Yes, I think I was trying to be a Hindu in part.

My first instinct as I came to was to touch my arm. I pushed back my sleeve expecting to see bruises. Of course, there were none. No material souvenirs from my travels to other realms. Some days I wish I had tangible proof that these roamings were more than just stored memories knitted together by my subconscious. Most days I am glad there is none.

Moisture on my lashes. Electricity in my veins. Something else too, more apparent for its absence. Lower back pain that had been a constant, staying with me even in sleep. Riding accidents, bad posture, contortions practising dentistry, pregnancy, a fall in the snow or two — a plausible explanation always at hand, I never paid it much heed. An SOS therapy when needed, then neglected once again.

'You carry the traumas of previous lives in your spine.' Unburdened at last, I was pain-free. Some truths perhaps need not be visibly veri-fied. Was I Hindu enough to accept that I had travelled back life-times, confronted the death of an unborn foetus, and made peace with it several births on? Usually, I would rush to discredit. This time I was more pragmatic.

'Energy can neither be created nor destroyed, only converted from one form to another.'

98

Albert Einstein, *Law of conservation of energy.*

What is the soul if not energy? And so, my soul can neither be created nor destroyed. When I die it cannot disappear into the ether. It is only logical, then, that it would take another form. Like water evaporating and condensing, maybe my soul vaporises only to rain as flesh once more. Who is to say the wind does not cast this vapour asunder? My essence travelling the globe and around again. Maybe there are familiar lands wherever I precipitate. Maybe these are my favourites. Who is to know?

A counter argument, the above all far-fetched. Abrupted life a metaphor for stolen innocence. Everything that follows merely a consequence. Yet I cannot explain away the pain that is no longer there. How it has disappeared after decades. Why now, not before, not later?

Thoughts gathering thick and heavy, I set off on my solace walk.

Royal Free Hospital. Grey. Cold. Soulless. Ugly. That was my first impression of this brutalist monstrosity fifteen years ago. Today, as I walk past the concrete behemoth that sullies my kitchen view, it is still grey and ugly. Not cold and soulless anymore. How could it be? It furnished my empty spaces with new life.

South End Green. I had read the Great Storm of 1987 flattened the wood here. Looking now, you couldn't tell. Even without their summer foliage, this new avenue of trees stands dense and tall, linking arms, waving a blustery welcome in the frosty winter air.

We share a kinship, the London Plane and me. Non-natives both, bound inextricably to the humus of this land. John Tradescant the Younger, a botanist, an explorer, is said to have carried back an American Sycamore and an Oriental Plane from his travels overseas. Planted side by side in his Vauxhall nursery garden they cross-pollinated and produced a hardy hybrid.

I think of our marriage like the Sycamore and the Plane. Branches laden with expectations, trunk thickened with pride, roots addled with resentment.

'Thank you for making dinner.'

'I'm sorry, I shouldn't have said that.'

'I hear you.'

Hand tucked in the crook of his arm. A kiss pressed to my hair. Toxins leach to the surface, shed like the bark of a Plane. Expunged, exposed, here we are. Not just him. Not just me. Us. Atypical, resilient, just like my London Plane.

Keats Grove. Slip of a road crowded thick with Victorian homes. Light filtering through curtained windows, halo of golden warmth. Halfway down, a Regency-style villa. Wide white frontage, tall Georgian windows, tidy front garden. Unexceptional in all but its name... Keats House. He spent a mere two years here, but it is said that in Wentworth Place (as it was once known) John Keats found inspiration, friendship and love. Short though it was, his time here was his most productive. Maybe he walked past this bent mulberry. Maybe it was not so bent then. Was it here that he conceived the words of *Ode to a Nightingale*?

In John Keats' plain garden, by his doubled-over tree, I saw my daughter toddle then take steady steps. It's how I navigated mother-hood, unsteady at first, then surer still.

'Take a picture Ma, of me and your poet's tree.' I tuck her hair behind her ear.

'We were not born for death, my immortal bird...'

Snap. I capture the moment.

Downshire Hill. Keats' legacy, not contained within his grove, spills out onto this wider road. I stop at Dante Gabriel Rossetti's once marital home. His early forays into poetry were said to be influenced by Keats. It is here that he lived with his muse, his love, his wife – Elizabeth Siddal. He buried his handwritten book of unpublished poems with her, nestled next to her head. I wonder what it would feel like to be the recipient of such passion. But later, he had her grave disinterred to retrieve his book.

Next door, fast forward a century, the tumultuous life and times of Peggy Ashcroft. An acting career that earned her a Damehood. Three troubled marriages that earned her the same number of divorces. My path had come so close to veering this way. Maybe this paradoxical placement, a daily walk past this polar positioning of love, steered me to the middle-ground.

'Sudden light I have been here before,
But how or when I cannot tell:
I know the grass beyond the door,
The sweet keen smell,
The sighing sound,
The light around the shore.'
Dante Gabriel Rossetti, *Sudden Light*.

I have been here before. I will return again. In this instance I inhabit the cautious middle. There will be another for reckless extremes. My own macabre romance awaits, of this, I am sure.

Keats Group Practice. Another red brick Victorian mansion block. A tape measure flopping from my burgeoning belly.

'Step on the scales, please.'

I am glad I can no longer see the needle swing, then settle.

A midwife jots down the readings. Gives the chart a once over, looks up with a pleasant smile.

'The numbers are increasing proportionately. She is growing beautifully. You are doing such a good job, well done.'

Stinging at the corners of my eyes, moisture threatening to spill.

Swallow past the lump in my throat, blink away the tears. Ache of inches, burn of kilos, all worthwhile. Finally, a love I am succeeding at. I was doing a good job, she said.

Hampstead High Street. A runway model, her lovely bones flipping look after look. From casual chic to avant-garde, her scent remains unchanged. Hit of coffee beans, cocoa powder; fresh baking, sweet raisin, cinnamon; lick of bergamot, stroke of galbanum. Lingering notes seep through the fabric I wear, permeating my pores. Her fragrance follows wherever I am, wafting from my cupboard of clothes, rising like steam from my skin.

Oriel Place. Cobbled urban garden, sequestered retreat. At its centre a solitary majestic Plane. Branches reaching for the face of the theatre above a pub.

'What's writing really about? It's about trying to take fuller possession of the reality of your life...' Ted Hughes may never have spoken these words when he read his poetry here at Léonie Scott-Matthews' hidden gem. Yet his words come rustling. Swoosh, swoosh, they brush by. I trace the Plane's calloused trunk, its bark beginning to split. Writing and all that came with it, allowed me to repossess a life that I had let drift.

Church Row. Familiar comfort and new discovery.

No. 27

George du Maurier lived here before moving onto Hampstead Grove. He returned in death. Some places are like that, they take hold.

'Sooner or later in the life of everyone comes a moment of trial. We

all of us have our particular devil who rides us and torments us, and we must give battle in the end.'
Daphne du Maurier, *Rebecca*.

I ponder his granddaughter's words on the way to my own battleground. I have laid many a siege here. Some days slain the devil, on others raised the flag. Walking away, not surrendering, returning to war another time.

No. 26

'I seem to have loved you in numberless forms, numberless times...
In life after life, in age after age, forever...'
Rabindranath Tagore, *Unending Love*.

My lips curl up in a smile. His context was different of course, but Tagore's words still ring true.

'Ma, Mama, Mummy...' she calls me by many a name. She could call me Lady if she wanted, and it would still surge through my being. I am her mother now, maybe she will be mine next. Perhaps we will be sisters, or the very closest of friends. I love her in every form, in life after life, in age after age, forever. I know why the blueprint of this place is imprinted in my veins. I am sure every dimension we visit must feel familiar in some way, but it is here that I learned to be her mum.

It feels like a pilgrimage, stopping at this black door with its unassuming fanlight. But for the time he spent here with Rothenstein, which saw his book of poems, *Gitanjali*, translated into English, I may never have read the words that are now embedded in my heart.

No. 17

Home of H. G. Wells. He moved here to stave off the storm of infidelity that threatened to flood his marriage. I hadn't anticipated storms or floods when I moved. They came all the same. Not in the form of infidelity to our union but infidelity to ourselves.

Wells and I may have divergent views on monogamy, but they do converge on the pointlessness of organised religion. Yet we both chose this place, fountainhead of our scepticism. Perhaps we fooled ourselves, the place chose us instead. The church, in particular its burial ground, a thorn in Wells' side. A stream of horse-drawn funeral processions kept his spirits sombre. Such irony then that he penned his greatest comic novel, *The History of Mr Polly*, while doused in thoughts of a depressive kind. He moved away soon after. I hope I never will.

Main churchyard, St John. I can see John Constable's tomb from where I stand. Plain, weathered, dull. Unremarkable, much like the reception his paintings received while he drew breath. Now as his body mingles with the soil of his favourite Hampstead, he is revered as one of the greats.

'I love every style and stump and lane in the village. As long as I can hold a brush, I will never cease to paint them.'

If I could paint, I would too. His paintings and these words still live but what of him? Is he John of another name, Constable of another place? Or is his brush laid to rest for good?

Additional Burial Ground, St John. Finally. The bosom of my solace. Once an open expanse traversed by hunter-gatherers, then a place where laundresses washed away the soil of humanity. Today, a resting place, earth washing away the soil of souls. Many an unpublished book nestled in their graves. My magnolia, she stands custodian of their tales, told and untold.

I pass by the grave of Eva Gore-Booth — poet, activist, champion of women's rights. She lies next to her partner, Esther Roper. Lifelong companions, they campaigned tirelessly for the women's suffrage movement. The nature of their relationship has been a subject of much speculation. Some claim that they were romantically involved, others that they merely cohabited. Labelling what they shared seems superfluous. They chose to be together in life and death. A love like that need not be named. Only craved.

Across, the Llewelyn Davies boys. Maybe such constancy is all that they would have wanted. Instead, Jim Barrie based his *Peter Pan and the Lost Boys* on them. Lost Boys, a telling choice. Their stories evoked a sense of wonder, bringing a twinkle to many an eye. For the boys themselves this mammoth fiction weighed heavy, snuffing out the twinkle of their youth. There have always been murmurings about the propriety of Barrie's connection with the boys, but there is no proof of anything untoward. Protectively, I wish these rumours away. Served the death of their parents at an early age, their plate was full enough without slapping on a side of abuse. Reunited as a family at last, they sleep now in the same tomb.

One wonders why their guardianship did not pass to their uncle by blood. Their mother's brother, Gerald du Maurier, who portrayed the villainous Captain Hook on stage for Barrie, lies in close proximity to their grave. As does their grandfather, George du Maurier, architect of the infamous Svengali. The best portrayal of this lothario is ascribed to Sir Herbert Beerbohm Tree, whose ashes lie only a few feet away. Grass tangles around their graves. Lives intertwined like its wild, green blades, bodies mingled like its roots. No longer George, Gerald, Herbert or the Lost Boys.

As the seasons roll over their crumbling stones, these names will disappear too. All that will remain are the words they wrote or were written of them. I look at the du Maurier headstone, distinct, memorable — a slab of timber slotted and pegged between two Celtic crosses, fittingly inscribed:

'A little trust that when we die, we reap our sowing and so goodbye.'
George du Maurier, *Trilby*.

In my forty-four years I have waved many a farewell. Some embedded in the lines of my palm. Some I haven't grasped quite yet.

One day it will be my turn. Despite my musings on this not being the end, I wish I knew for sure. But then I think it is better that I don't. This place has opened its gates, shared its secrets with me. Where was I yesterday? Where will I be tomorrow? In the end, maybe all that matters is that I am here today.

These abstractions keep me coming back to my magnolia. Duelling with feeble rays, she and the sun tussling like two stags locking horns. The sun retreats, leaving her winner for a day, or two, maybe more. Magnolia won't stand forever. Another will take her place and so the cycle carries on.

'Mama, where is my PE kit?'
Ring, ring... hubby calling. (2) missed calls.
'Ma I can't reach the towel.'
Buzz... 'Delivery.'
Ring, ring... 'You never pick up your phone!'
'Mummy what's for breakfast?'
'I can't find my car keys. Did I leave them upstairs?'
'Let me check.'
'Mummy where is my spelling book?'
Ring, ring... 'Did you find the keys?'
'Give me a minute.' Call ended.
'Ouch!' A pair of barbed velvet paws find skin instead of flailing pyjama bottoms.
Ring, ring.

I bundle them out the door. Look at the phone discarded on the bed. 8:30 am. Lay back, soaking up silence as fleeting as the London sun. Turn my face into the sheets, still warm. Buried in their rumpled creases, the scent of Fairy Liquid, cedarwood, peonies, bubblegum and us.

To Armenia and Back

The Paradox of Exile

Pauline Hallam Mason

'I should like to see any power of the world destroy this race, this small tribe of unimportant people, whose wars have all been fought and lost, whose structures have all crumbled, literature is unread, music is unheard, and prayers are no more uttered. Go ahead destroy this race. Let us say that it is again 1915. There is war in the world. Destroy Armenia. See if you can do it. Send them from their homes into the desert. Let them have neither bread nor water... See if they will not live again. See if they will not laugh again.' [1]

Seven o'clock in the morning, September 1999, waiting at the airport for a visa to enter Armenia, the stink of kerosene, used on the floors, strong in my nostrils. We've flown from New York to London, London to Vienna and finally here to Yerevan, the capital. Driving into the city the rising sun lights up shabby stalls and rundown shacks, often with a dog chained outside. Under a tree's spreading branches, a man grilling joints of lamb, his flock around him grazing on the meagre grass. Hanging from the tree,

---

1. William Saroyan, *Inhale and Exhale,* (NY: Random House, 1936), 438. A version of this quote is displayed in many museums and churches in Armenia.

lamb carcasses butchered for sale. A disturbing first glimpse of the city.

This was the Caucasus, about which I had romantic ideas. Mount Ebruz and the tribes of Persians and Tartars conjured up an image of adventure to me. The reality that first day is a shock. Reaching a grim, Soviet-style apartment block, walking through a courtyard past old people and small children, all dressed in rags. Some selling small, worthless items and others holding out dirty hands for money. That first day we have no Armenian coins and we'd been warned not to give them money. The lifts aren't working so we climb six flights of crumbling stairs with our luggage. Passing the rubbish chutes on each landing is an ordeal, the stench of rotting food, the flies buzzing around. Inside the apartment we find dirty cupboards in the kitchen, filthy floors in every room, a disgusting cake of soap, covered in black hairs, lying in the bathroom.

I was in mid-life transformation and a new career. I was determined to forge a different shape to my life. I would be teaching at the Yerevan Linguistic University with a group of Americans, including my partner, John. He'd accepted a Fellowship from the Open Society to lecture there, and I looked forward to the experience. This was not a good start to the adventure. I felt tired and dispirited. 'I can't stay here,' I thought.

We started to clean the rooms, beginning in the kitchen, making it inhabitable until we found somewhere better to live. The doorbell rang; it was a young man from the internet provider. He looked startled seeing John on his knees, scrubbing the kitchen floor, but began to instruct him how to connect our laptop to the internet. 'I don't know anything about all that,' said John. 'Tell my partner!' The man looked at him in disbelief but gave me the information. After he left, still looking bewildered, we laughed and felt better.

I needed to adjust to this different society. The orientation we attended at Yale University included a lecture on the long history of Armenia, a Christian country since the 4th century AD.

After the reign of Tigran the Great, their Golden Period, which ended in 95BC, their history is one of grief and loss of homeland and territory, with genocide in 1915.[2] The result, a people deeply passionate about keeping hold of their remaining land, identity, and language.[3] Feelings passed down through the generations at home and abroad. For the diaspora, living far away, it is strongly held as an ideal although few of them have visited the country. For seventy-five years Armenia was under Russian rule. Then, in 1991, when the Soviet Empire fell, Armenia declared itself an independent republic. With independence came a decline in industry, a disastrous earthquake and fierce fighting over the corridor to Nagorno-Karabakh.

I understood that we were going to a poor country with a long and difficult history. But nothing prepared me for the feelings of disgust and shock I felt that day.

***

Old women, bent over short-handled brooms sweep the dusty streets of Yerevan. Others sit on doorsteps chopping fresh green herbs for sale.

Suddenly, sharp, spicy smells in the air: the indoor market. Tables covered with mounds of ground yellow turmeric, brown cumin, orange chilli and black pepper. Piles of exotic fruit, persimmons, pomegranates and peaches, heaps of red and green peppers, purple aubergines, enormous radishes and pale cabbages.

At the end of the street, Mount Ararat, lost to Armenia, snow cap shining, ethereal, floats above the city.

***

That afternoon we walked along the shabby back streets towards the

---

2. Over a million Armenians were forcibly removed from their land in 1915 by the Turks. Some were killed and others died as they crossed the desert without food or water.
3. The Armenian alphabet is unique. It was designed by St. Mashtots in the 5th century to translate the bible.

centre of the city. After the market we came into the main square, its Italianate buildings of golden tufa stone glowing in the sun. There were banks, restaurants, and the Marriot Armenia Hotel, where I longed to book a room, but knew it would be expensive. Taxis braked, buses pulled in and left, people were shopping, strolling, eating. Beyond the square we found parks and a broad, tree-lined street. Here were the embassies, the university, the Parliament, and the concert hall. A huge statue of Mother Armenia stood on a hill overlooking the whole city. She'd replaced Stalin when his bronze statue was dismantled after independence.

There were around a hundred and fifty westerners in the city, mainly British and North American, there to help with the transition to democracy, in practical ways as well as teaching. This included repairing the pipes bringing water to the city and helping to create a constitution and a legal system.

Our group of lecturers was funded by the Open Society Institute, and we were warmly welcomed by staff and students. One morning, we were invited to meet the staff at the university. The President, Tigran Vasaryan, gave a formal speech declaring that he, the staff, and the students were grateful for our presence. Then brandy and chocolates were passed round, not my first choice at eleven o'clock in the morning, so tiny sips and a hand over the glass when seconds came around. I was sitting next to the President. He turned to me and shook my hand,

'I suppose this is your first visit to Armenia?' he inquired.

'Yes, and it's um... interesting to be here.'

'Oh, but Yerevan is nothing. You must see the mountains, lakes and ancient monasteries to really know our country.'

'Yes, that would be marvellous. I've always wanted to see the Caucasus mountains, Mount Ebruz and...'

My face was red as he explained I was mistaken, that mountain isn't in Armenia. However, he expounded at length on the beauty of the Armenian countryside and the general excellence of Armenia compared to anywhere else in the world.

I nodded and smiled, breathing a sigh of relief when he turned to his neighbour on the other side. Everyone was friendly, but we didn't learn much about them personally, in that formal setting.

Along with the teaching we were expected to provide a cultural background through outreach. John and I both owned a large number of books, so we decided to set up a library. We arranged for British Airways to bring over a thousand books on history, philosophy, feminist theory, literature, and poetry.

After the customs officer reluctantly released them, we donated them to the university. A room with shelves was found and the language students were delighted to have the opportunity to borrow them. Then we set up a weekly film club, which both lecturers and students enjoyed.

I discovered that the English Literature students were reading old-fashioned books, for example, the Forsyte Saga. So, I decided to teach the modernists: Virginia Woolf, James Joyce, and T. S. Eliot. I planned a syllabus and had it approved by the English Department Head, Marine Gasparian. She asked eagerly if she could read the books herself and perhaps sit in on some of the classes, and of course I agreed.

The classroom was full of old desks with inkwells, reminding me of my first infant school in 1940s England. I pushed some to the back of the room and we set the rest in a horseshoe shape in front of my larger desk, which I often sat on rather than behind. My aim was to create a relaxed atmosphere far removed from the rote learning which the students were used to.

At first, they were reluctant to speak, but by the end of term we had some very good, sometimes heated discussions. The Head of the Department came twice, and then, satisfied that all was well, left us alone. That helped to relax the pupils. They were all English language students in their second or third year and spoke good, very correct English.

About twenty-five students had been attending the classes, so when the time for end of term exams arrived, I set out the desks and asked the office to print my questions. On the morning of the exams, I found a dozen additional students standing around looking confused. They said they had signed up for the class and had come to take the exam.

I told them to wait and made straight for the Head's office. I told her what had happened, and she shrugged.

'Yes, I'm afraid that's normal. These people are registered so you must let them take the exam.'

I couldn't believe what I was hearing but waited for the extra papers to be printed. Back in the classroom, more desks had been set out and the newcomers sat in a row at the back. As they hadn't answered my carefully phrased questions, I failed them all. Three days later a tearful young woman waited outside the door for me.

'I failed the exam, so I won't get my grant next term. I have a child, and I couldn't get a babysitter, but I must finish this degree.'

'You must talk to Miss Gasparian, she has the results.'

I found out later that all those students, who only came that day, were given a pass grade by the Department Head. Another puzzling feature of this society.

We found our apartment on Pushkin Street, near to the university, when I met a musician at an International Women's Club lunch. She had a pianist friend who was leaving to work for two years in Moscow, and he wanted tenants who would look after his grand piano. We met him, liked the apartment, assured him we would care for the instrument and signed the agreement. This was our home for the next two years. Up two flights of wide, stone stairs, the rooms were clean and well-furnished. There was also a water storage system, as we only had running water for two hours in the morning and the same in the evening. From our bedroom window we saw Ararat golden at dawn and disappearing into the mist at dusk.

I take the pottery pomegranate between my hands, a crystal ball.

The shiny, red glaze glows and where it splits dark seeds spill out.

Vivid, cinematic scenes appear.

Spellbound, I see mountains, waterfalls, rivers and lakes in the wild Caucasus. I lie on the ropes between the twin hulls of the catamaran on Lake Sevan, listening to the sad story of Tamar, who swam from the island monastery at night to meet his lover. One night, she lit the lamp and waited. He drowned and she, drowned in tears, cried 'Ahk Tamar' to the unforgiving water.

Half term holiday came, and we were taken to a hotel on the lake for progress meetings with our director. When these were over, we visited the monastery built in 874 AD on the island, now a peninsula because the water level has fallen. The statue of Tamar's lover reaching out to the lake stands there, and a cemetery full of khachkars, the ornately carved, sandstone crosses. After the hot, dusty city, this mountainous countryside surrounding blue-green water was deeply refreshing.

Driving on the country roads, we saw the remnants of Armenia's agricultural past. In the late afternoon, we were surrounded by a large flock of sheep and a shepherd delivering the animals to their various owners in the village, after a day grazing on the hillsides.

Yerevan University held a reception at the Sergei Paradjanov Museum and the visiting lecturers were invited. I was introduced to a Professor of Ancient Armenian History, a small, lively man, not young, with receding hair. He told me the story behind the museum, his dark eyes twinkling and his mobile face showing all his emotions.

Paradjanov was a filmmaker who upset the Communist authorities with his film, 'The Colour of Pomegranates'. Forbidden to make films, he made collage scenes and framed them in wooden boxes which cover the walls of his house. I was captivated by my informant's vibrant personality and knew that John should meet him too.

From that night on, Professor Eduard Danielyan became our

guide and friend. We saw Armenia through his geographical and historical knowledge. He took us hiking to see ruined Greek temples and monasteries built in the early days of Armenia's conversion to Christianity in the 4th century AD.

We went with him in search of the ruins of Ashtarat, the ancient capital, planned according to Plutarch, by Hannibal and built in 176 BCE. Eduard hadn't found the ruins yet when we strayed too near the Turkish border and saw a line of tall watchtowers, each with an armed soldier. After a warning shot was fired, we were rescued by a gentle Kurdish shepherd who led us quickly out of danger.

I was surprised that Eduard was so friendly with this man. I'd read that Kurds were helping the Turks to evict the Armenians from their land in 1915.

'You don't understand,' was the response we frequently heard from Eduard. He explained that the Kurds had been forced to assist with the genocide and that they had apologised to the Armenians. Our saviour and his fellow villagers left Turkey and lived peacefully as farmers in Armenia.

Eduard loved art, music, and poetry, alongside his passionate love for his beleagured nation. He often stated that Armenia was 'the cradle of civilisation'. This comment refers to the first Armenia, which was part of the fertile crescent of the Euphrates region.

Vassily Grossman, a Russian author, wrote of the Armenian poet Martirosyan, '*More than anything in the world he loves his nation. What matters is the global, even cosmic, superiority of the Armenian people.*'[4]

This exactly describes Eduard's attitude. He firmly believed in the superiority of the Armenian race which he felt was proven by their survival after removal from their original homeland, enemy occupation and genocide.

On October 27th, 1999, we walked into a cafe and, instead of

4. John W. Mason, 'Living in the Lie: The Armenian Intelligentsia in the Soviet Union', Oral History Society, Autumn 2005, Vol.3, No.2

the news in colour, we saw the ballet, Swan Lake, in black and white, on the television. Eduard had told us that this happened whenever a tragic incident occurred. After our coffee we went to the university to find classes cancelled. Students and staff stood around looking shocked.

'Whatever has happened?' John asked Eduard, who was in the office we shared.

'Assassins came into Parliament with guns under their coats. They shot Sargsiyan, the Prime Minister, the Speaker and six other politicians. John, you don't realise, this is a terrible thing for our country.' He was almost in tears.

'I certainly do know, Eduard,' said John, 'and I'm sorry.'

The rumours were that this was a conspiracy led by the authoritarian President Robert Kocharyan, and there was a suspicion that the guards had been bribed to allow the murderers in with their guns. Whoever enabled the killings, this was a huge setback for Armenia's emerging democracy. One more loss to be mourned by the Armenians.

The shop windows were draped in black, and the streets were full of sad-eyed people on the day of the funerals. A solemn cortege passed along the streets to the cemetery, the pavements lined with citizens dressed in black and openly weeping. The newspaper was printed with black borders and when Eduard translated the headlines for us, the assassinations were all the news there was for a week or so. There was going to be an investigation to find out who planned and enabled this shooting, but although the five assassins were caught and imprisoned, the whole story never came out. This traumatic event was quietly buried.

Solemn, carrying flowers, crowds walk uphill, kneel and place offerings around the Shield of the Eternal Flame.

Praying, they look up to the slender Obelisk, moving on as hundreds more perform the same oblation.

Soldiers march slowly beating drums, the duduk's continuous tone hovers, deep, funereal.
Grief and loss, heavy, dragging, incurable.

The following year, on April 24th, annual National Holiday for Genocide Victims Remembrance Day, we went with Eduard to the ceremony at the Memorial Museum and Monument, on Tsitzamak-aberd Hill.

Although it was a moving experience, it also puzzled me. In spite of their everyday struggles with poverty the Armenians put a lot of energy and money into their grief for the dead and their lost lands. I learnt that much of the money spent came from the diaspora, who were the main supporters of these events. John brought money over for relatives in Yerevan, from an American academic, who had never visited himself.

I have since discovered many books by sons and daughters of the diaspora living in Europe or America. Books of poetry, of autobiography and of biography. A doctor in America has recently self-published a book of poetry and paintings titled *Dreams of Armenia*[5], encapsulating the diasporian feeling perfectly. The first eponymous poem begins:

I wish I was born there
Instead of a stranger's land
A part of me will never be
And I will never know
What it's like to leave a homeland.
I wish I spoke the language
Another one was taught instead
And I grew up with a strange tongue.
Wishing I could go there

---

5. Ashot Kotcharian, *Dreams of Armenia*, (Independently published, 2021).

And make that place my homestead
And yet I do not go
Maybe I'm worried
Of being a stranger
In my own homeland
Where my ancestors are buried

With Eduard we visited Nagorno-Karabakh, then the Armenian enclave in Azerbaijan, during a time of fragile and uneasy peace.

Entering the Armenian lands, we stopped to look down at the white stone Ghazanchetstots Cathedral, recently restored after bomb damage during the war. Nearing the Armenian capital, Stepanakert, we saw a cemetery with photographs on the headstones of young men killed in the fighting.

Rooms had been arranged for us in a large farmhouse. Sitting on the terrace in the evening, with a glass of golden wine, we enjoyed the view of the distant mountains. Then Emira Gabrielyan, our hostess, pointed to large holes in the stone walls. They were shell holes from the Azeri guns. She told us that her husband had died of a heart attack during one bombardment. After this reminder of the war she had suffered we no longer wanted to see the mountains of Azerbaijan and went quietly to bed. Nearly all the Armenians have now been driven out of Nagorno-Karabakh, as the Russian peacekeepers stood by.[6] I wonder what happened to Emira, if she is still alive.

---

6. Nathalie Tocci, 'Nargorno-Karabakh's tragedy has echoes of Europe's dark past. But a remedy lies in Europe too', theguardian.com, 2 October 2023. https://www. theguardian.com/commentisfree/2023/oct/02/nagorno-karabakhs-tragedy-has-echoes-of-europes-dark-past-but-a-remedy-lies-in-europe-too

Leaning on the iron railing, watching tumbling water, trucks passing on the dusty road sway, hurrying to market, pomegranates falling behind them.

'I can't understand those Georgians,' says the Armenian student.

'Neither can they understand you. Blame monk Mashtots — he invented your languages.'

He shrugs. 'We all speak English now.'

This strange and beautiful country takes me, holds me in thrall, and these dark-eyed, eager students, now beginning their own lives, forget their country's oppression. Their mothers, fathers, grandparents, remember genocide, Turks, Russians, communism.

Western democracy has not yet brought the promised good.

After two years living and teaching in Armenia, we knew that our time there was finished. I could see that the future did not look hopeful for those living in Armenia. A large proportion of the population in the city were living well below the poverty line. Many were looking back at the Communist period as a time of prosperity and full employment. Armenia's time as a Soviet Republic was not the same as that of the 'captive nations' of Eastern Europe.[7]

In 1920, as the Turkish army followed the genocide by attempting to seize Armenia's remaining territory, the Russian army stopped them. So, the Russians were seen as saviours. Then, the progress represented by becoming an industrial rather than an agricultural economy had fuelled Armenian nationalism.[8]

In spite of all that I had learnt from Eduard, I still couldn't help feeling that the Armenians should try to get on with their life in a democracy and move on from the past. Even though I couldn't see

---

7. Vaclav Havel, *The Power of the Powerless*, (NY: M. E. Sharpe, 1985).
8. John W. Mason, 'Living in the Lie: The Armenian Intelligentsia in the Soviet Union', Oral History Society, Autumn 2005, Vol.3, No.2

why they continually reminded the world of their past history, I felt compassion for them. Often returning from Britain or America I felt depressed, until the cheerful smiles and dark good looks of the people I saw every day helped me to forget.

After five years in the capitals of three post-Soviet countries, fresh, unpolluted air would be good for us. We arranged to spend at least a year in Maine in a rented farmhouse overlooking an inlet of the sea. I looked forward to teaching for the University of Maine. Also, it would be wonderful to have access to the sea, supermarkets and running hot and cold water all day. However, we had made many friends in Armenia and there were aspects of our life there that I would miss.

One weekend, we visited a Greek temple at Garni, which had stood on that site for at least two millennia. I felt the power of this ancient land seeping into my bones and my mind. I had seen much larger and better preserved temples in Greece, along with several hundred other tourists. But standing here, between the columns with no tour guides, only Eduard and a few friends, was a totally different experience, which I shall never forget.

During our last few days Eduard and his colleagues organised a farewell picnic for the western lecturers. The day started with a drive to the summit of Mount Aragats, now the highest mountain in Armenia. By a frozen lake, watching young people skating or just sliding about on the thick ice, shivering, we drank Armenian schnapps. Then, back down to a sunlit valley with a fast-flowing river. Sitting outdoors we ate *ishkav*, trout, caught in the river and cooked in deep holes in the ground. On the barbeque were pork chops, aubergines, and dolmas. Salad and the thin sheets of *layash*, bread, completed the feast. Toasts to the future, with pledges to keep in touch, were drunk with red wine. I knew I was going to miss these dear people.

'*we can tear bread, pour oil, sprinkle salt*
and watch him close his eyes to the smoke

of aubergine, the sharpness of strained yoghourt. [9]

A sinuous snake slithers into my psyche.
I struggle, force it under the heel of my shoe.
The coils slip, silently, slowly back.
Despair and loss smother me.
Through the mist of misery, I see the sun on tree and hill.
I cannot recover my joy.

In the two decades since we left Armenia, I have lived mostly in America. One summer morning, in 2003, we sat in a cafe in Salamanca, Spain and John called his sister in America. His mother had died and two days later we were in New Jersey to be with the family. The other three siblings had their own homes, so finally it was proposed that we stay, at least temporarily, to caretake the ten-acre property, until it was sold. The land was beautiful, a wooded area with a deep ravine, where they'd found Native American arrowheads. I agreed because of that word 'temporarily', I hadn't thought we'd stay in the country.

After the sale, John wanted to stay and teach in America, and I was happy to continue teaching online and going to my annual faculty meetings in Maine. We bought a house in Virginia with a few acres, the taxes were reasonable and the countryside beautiful.

I began to translate and edit the memoir of a heroic Armenian woman, who spent years in Stalin's gulag. I made it clear that this new life would only be possible for me if I could go regularly across the Atlantic to visit family and friends. John agreed, as he has family in Britain and Europe. We said we'd stay for maybe five years, made

9. Sarah Mnatzaganian, *Lemonade in the Armenian Quarter,* (Against the Grain Press, 2022).

friends, settled in, and stayed for twenty. We occasionally met some of our American colleagues from Armenia and Eduard came to America every summer for his two-week holiday until he died in 2017. We also undertook regular editing work for him.

A year or two ago I sat at my desk noticing the pottery pomegranate, given to me by Eduard, glowing on my window ledge. As I considered my time in Armenia, I saw not one but two countries side by side. One the post-Soviet democratic republic working hard to restore its security and financial stability. The other a nation of peoples looking back to their past lands and yearning to be there again, which is a total impossibility. As I look at the black seeds spilling out of the pomegranate my thoughts are dark and despairing.

I long to be in England, where nobody comments on my accent, where I'm not likely to get shot in the supermarket and most important, where my family live. I want to get a train to London and see a play at the Almeida or an exhibition at the National Gallery. To visit family living from Cornwall to Scotland. To visit friends in Cambridge. To stay again in the windmill at Cley-Next-the Sea in Norfolk. Green lawns, bare mountains, rocky cliffs on the coasts. My native island calls to me. Maybe I long to return to a place which only exists in my imagination, as the original Armenia only now exists in the imaginations of its people.

I am torn in two, a rabbit caught in the headlights not knowing which way to move. There is no solution. My home, my books, family possessions are all here, transported from their origins as I am. Most of all, my love is here, with whom I have spent thirty years of adventure and homemaking. I can't leave without him and he won't leave.

Lone as the pine, talk myself out, try to be,
the mirror argues like a weeping willow

that island stands for a remote and longed for place[10]
What chains hold me here? I find no solid rock
feel wildcat fury, passion.
King Solomon's wisdom will not solve this puzzle.
Lengthways or across, legless or pegleg,
headless, heartless.
With you and not here is the goalpost I can never reach alive.

I never fully understood the Armenians' passion for their lost
country when I lived there. Now this longing has become a personal
emotion for me. A quarter of a century later, I recognise the symp-
toms as my own. Now I begin to feel its strong hold.

I know that my country is not 'the promised land'; there are
many economic and social problems, many unwelcome changes. As
a child in wartime and post-war Britain I didn't find it a good place
to be. Instead, I buried myself under a great weight of literature and
poetry. I lived in another world and that's the world I long for now.
I know this when I'm being rational and practical. Then a strong
passion returns, pulling me back to my roots.

The emotion gnaws at me, agitates me, destroys my peace.
Those dispossessed Armenians had no choice, they were starving,
homeless and oppressed. Those that survived the killing were sent
out across the desert with no water, and many more died on the
way. Clothed, fed and free, I had the choice and became a willing
exile. A feeling so pervasive cannot be rationalised. Perhaps there is a
universal trait in humans to long for more. Exiles, both forced and
voluntary, wishing they were elsewhere.

10. Adam Nicolson, *How To Be: Life Lessons from the Early Greeks,* (UK: Harper-
Collins, 2023).

The Road Home

R. L. Shelley

My parents modestly might have described their life as ordinary, focusing on work, family, and friends and fulfilling society and family expectations. It's impossible to ignore their immense courage, uprooting from Italy and moving to Australia after World War II. Circumstances beyond people's control often dictate such life-altering decisions.

As I remembered our family's stories, I began sifting through old photographs and thinking about them. A vivid narrative of their first years in Australia emerged. They would have laughed if I had told them this story was a tribute to them, insisting that they had done nothing unusual.

Weathering some incredibly challenging times, toiling tirelessly in work that seemed impossibly difficult and in a country that did not always extend a warm welcome, they never faltered. Their dream was simple — a fresh beginning in a small corner of northern Australia they could call home. An Italian community was already established and thriving there, with similar people who successfully had made this place their home. It was their turn to follow those before them. The journey is a testament to their resilience and a story that must be told.

I visited my birthplace, Ingham, in far North Queensland, for the first time in June 2019 — a long time since my birth in 1954. Mom and Dad warned me off visiting many times, always for the same dismissive reason: the place was not worth the trip. I believed them, but age has a way of changing your mind. I was not sure how I would feel about the visit now.

This was particularly true considering what I was told during my lively talks with Dad just before his passing. His voice and expressions had always hinted at tensions within the family and unease with Ingham. I never wanted to press him on those emotional conversations.

My visit purposely coincided with the yearly Australian Italian festival, celebrating the contributions of Italian immigrants to the local community. I'm not sure I entirely agreed with the cheesy, cliché Italian food and festivities. Who knew deep-fried pizza was a thing? But I understood a community's desire to relive a romanticised past, even if it was just memories of an idealised time.

Toobanna is a small hamlet just outside Ingham, where we lived. Optimistically, I was hoping to find the family shack, but I knew the twenty-first century would have caught up with the place. The old houses were long gone, sadly replaced with a flat, featureless landscape, with nearly every tree and open space now fields of sugar cane. A major road divided the village, slicing the vibrant, dense community I remembered so fondly as a child, where men would gather in each other's yards after work and talk incessantly about today, tomorrow and the future; women would talk about the important things; children would play with freshly cut stalks of burnt cane, bending them till they dripped fresh sugar nectar. But I did admire those who lived and worked beneath the relentless sun.

The Queensland cane fields were where people laughed, fought, worked, and socialised together as they breathed the air thick with sugary perfume, a tangible testament to the oppressive humidity that clings to every leaf and blade of grass, distorting everything with its intense heat.

Uninspiring, newish houses now sporadically lined both sides, with cane fields interleaved between. Dirt road, now bitumen-paved, leading from one cane field to another; single-storey houses, ill fit for an area prone to flooding every other season. There was a reason a 'Queenslander' was a well-established architectural style, with houses raised high above the flood level on timber stilts. Everything missing now.

Elizabeth Gilbert *(Eat, Pray, Love)* was right when she described Venice as a city in a Bergman film; you can admire it but don't want to live there. I had the same feeling about Ingham, a town so indentured to sugar cane and, like all single-industry towns, with no reason to exist beyond its primary function.

I wanted to hug Rosy; everyone important to me had died. She was my last human contact with Ingham. Rosy typified the northern Italian *Nonna*, an immensely proud woman in her mid-eighties who exuded confidence in her robust appearance and quiet, authoritative speech. I had only met Rosy a few dozen times over the years, but never in Ingham until this visit. I had formed a bond with someone I thought I hardly knew, but my Mom and Dad's close friend was the last remaining holder of pieces of memories of my family and their life in Queensland. I likened it to those little chunks of Roman tesserae found in the grass fields, in danger of being dug up and erased forever.

I sat with Rosy that quiet June afternoon on the patio at her house on the coast at Lucinda, espresso in hand, overlooking the Coral Sea. The fields had been good to her and her family. Although retired, she still helped run the huge cane farms her sons now operated.

I listened intently, absorbing every word. I couldn't help thinking of the stories finally being laid flat; most of them I knew, but the missing pieces began to make sense. She spoke of my dad, Elio, and my mom, Lina, so fondly that, for a moment, I forgot how strained some of our days together had been. We spoke for a long time. I feverishly filed the stories away in my memory.

It was 1948. At twenty-two years of age and with no prospects in post-war Europe, my father, Elio and his brother Otto emigrated to Australia on the Lloyd Triestino, SS *Toscana*. It had been a passenger liner converted to a troop carrier and back again, so the basic comforts were there. A month-long journey passed slowly as anxiety and anticipation of a new land filled their thoughts. As much as the blue ocean was unrelenting and never-ending, they believed there were things to look forward to in the unknown.

Australia was always a country of confusion with varying policies on immigration from Europe, particular Italy. Pressure applied from existing enclaves of Italians firmly established in North Queensland as far back as the late 19th century, only served to add to the muddle.

The lack of general workers, cane cutters and the nervousness of Australians to accept immigrants who were not that long ago enemy combatants, together with the newly released interned Italian Australians, made for a confusing time for both communities. It was inevitable that some immigrants brought with them incompatible ideologies and a lingering suspicion of old enemies. War is war, and no one escapes without consequences.

Italians, particularly from northern Italy, made good settlers before the war, though some undesirable types inevitably got in. As a people, they were considered industrious and took kindlier than most to climate and other conditions in the cane fields.

Despite the apparent difficulties, Australia promised a new life divorced from the chaos of post-war Europe. For young, single men, it promised the adventure of a lifetime. There was a pact made amongst themselves to find purpose in their lives in an unknown land, only spoken of in whispers back home lest people think it madness. Many Italians journeyed to this remote country, some emigrating to the big cities to try their luck, and some to farming communities so familiar to them back in Italy. Some just decided to seek their fortunes in the cane fields of FNQ.

The fields are called 'Far North Queensland', never just North Queensland. It simply acknowledged that they were a long way away from anywhere, including from anywhere in Australia, or that FNQ was a strange place in the fifties, remote, distinct, and isolated. Still, the lure of money and potential success proved irresistible to many.

Cane cutting in Queensland in the 1950s saturated the senses. Dense, oppressive humidity filled the lungs with nothing but water. Cane fields were burnt and blackened to drive out rats and native taipan snakes and to protect cane cutters from razor-sharp leaves. Cutters only had their wits and the cane knife, a custom, long-handled, short-bladed, sharp tool to protect themselves. They would buy their blade at the hardware store and fashion the handle to suit themselves. Many a time, a reluctant snake was dispatched with one blow.

It was 1953. A gentle, northerly breeze stirred the thick, sweet grass in the early evening. Elio smelled the burnt cane. It had that distinct odour of caramel cooked for too long, syrupy and smoky. He stood on the rough wooden balcony of his Queenslander, hands tightly clenched on the wooden handrail. This was as he had done every sunset and through every season.

He stared, motionless, beyond his yard boundary into the distance. The last wisps of smoke rose against the dying, yellow light of sunset. From the burnt cane, flecks of black fell from the night sky. It would be his and his gang's field tomorrow, and he knew they had their work cut out. Time here was measured in seasons, work schedules, money, and sweat. There were no days, hours, or minutes.

Elio had left everything in Italy for this. The fading shades of shadowed light gave him food for thought as the nights fell again and again. He had forgotten for a moment where he was, and before tomorrow, there would be a little peace as he felt the times changing as relationships and work grew harder. His body shuddered with anticipation in the 38-degree heat. Lina stood on the balcony and stared blankly at him. She knew she didn't want to be here. Elio stayed silent.

As he arrived home each day, Lina would see the ash on his face, the filthy clothes, and the air of satisfied exhaustion. The black ash stuck to him and the others, blending all cutters into bizarre, indistinguishable, silhouetted characters from a Japanese bunraku show.

'*The dirt and ash and bristles of burnt cane get into your clothes and your hair and skin. You wash twice a day.*'[1]

Lina waited patiently each day, with food prepared, never saying much. My mother was fearless when using words, but she was scared of their meanings and what Dad thought of her. Days stretched into nights. He was too tired to talk.

He didn't hate Lina for not wanting to stay. He understood the harshness of the place, the loneliness, and the isolation during the day. He certainly had no delusions about it.

By the third year, life had taken its toll on her. Heated discussions always revolved around why they were here, and the answer always remained the same: 'I like it here.' She instinctively knew it was his way of not answering the question.

Dad lived in and around Como, Lombardy, in northern Italy, for much of his early life. He never sought beauty in life or work but wished for a simple existence. He searched for a calm that was never to be in post-war Italy but found purpose in hard work; after all, a dedicated work ethic was what he was brought up to believe was the only worthy pursuit. Two brothers took a different path and remained in Italy, the third accompanied him, and his fourth brother died in the war.

The old country didn't mean much to him anymore. Clinging

---

1. https://www.youtube.com/watch?v=_2D3ioAH6_4

to the past served no purpose. He didn't entirely reject the old values; some were too deep-rooted. Religion did not play an essential part in his life, but, as a Catholic, some things would never leave him, bringing comfort when he needed it.

When he arrived in 1948, he lived in a boarding house with similar men. At a communal table, they all gathered for their meals, each taking turns to cook and to discuss all manner of things, but mostly about work and opportunities. The rudimentary accommodation's corrugated steel walls and roof kept some water out but little else. Elio understood the freedom of living and working outside. He had done so back in Italy. He never understood the allure of crowded, oppressive cities.

He worked the fields wherever men were needed. Elio and his mates signed contracts with the local co-op that guaranteed a good price for their toil.

'If you cut cane with a man, you soon find out what he's like. A good mate is a good mate.'

Elio was to be a 'top ganger', able to attract and surround himself with the best cutters who could rely on him to find the best working conditions and pay. However, the relentless repetitiveness of this work, and responsibility, made it challenging to find a stable life outside the cane fields.

In 1952, he married Lina in a typical Italian ceremony in St Patrick's Church, Ingham, followed by a reception at the Royal Hotel. They had met at the Royal a year before.

As a twenty-year-old, Lina never sought or wished to follow any particular belief in life, being content, even at that early age, to be led by others who, in her opinion, knew more than she did. She was more capable than that, but constantly wrestled with her reality, consumed by her duty to respect old Italian family values as they were and always would be. She needed to escape the oppressive heat, humidity, and demanding family in a new country.

The decision to emigrate wasn't hers but her brother's. She arrived in 1950. Lina hadn't been in Ingham all that long when she was confronted by two snakes while on her way to the outhouse. She decided she was leaving. It didn't matter where, she said, 'Just not here!' It made her question why she had followed the family. The old values of Italy began to seem as distant as Italy was from Queensland.

Mom never saw the fields as Dad did. In the first year of marriage, they provided some comfort and a welcome respite away from the chaos of Italy. By the second year, she glared at them with resentment. She now saw them as vast fields of unfulfilled promises of happiness. She saw the men returning as all the same; ash-blackened caricatures of people, all flawed, with the same stupid ideals and goals of money and success, whatever that meant.

Elio and Lina began to appear to have a normal life. There was talk of starting a family, a future for all, and a way out. Elio promised to consider giving up cane cutting for a new life in the city. For her, there was nowhere to go. Lina felt trapped. She was fashioning her life around her immediate family and friends.

My uncle Gianni emigrated in May 1949 on the *SS Napoli*. As the eldest, he was responsible for setting up a beachhead for the family to follow. His mother, father and sister, Lina, arrived in 1950 on the *SS Surriento*. The ravages of war had also forced them out of Italy. Australia promised a better future away from their dire economic circumstances in Europe.

Mom died in 2017. A year passed before I could sit with Dad and talk through things. I pulled a small photo out and pointed to me sitting in the back of a ute on the Queensland property with other relatives gathered around for a 'formal' photo. Not that anything was that formal up there; maybe Saturday 'formal' dance nights at the pub. He did smile. That was the moment when it all became clear to him. He couldn't stop talking after that. I was reminded of a line from *Field Guide to Getting Lost* by Rebecca Solnit: 'Sometimes an old photograph, an old friend, an old letter will remind you that you are not who you once were.'

Looking at the photo, I had to agree I wasn't, and neither were the others. Dad talked about Gianni as if he regretted ever knowing him. Gianni had always admired Mussolini. Even occasional praise of the man in polite dinner conversation greatly annoyed Dad, fearing that his attitude had a more than passing effect on those around him. He spoke of Gianni's ability to manipulate Lina into doing and acting in a way that only made sense to my uncle.

Those first conversations with Dad were him recalling sensory memories, sometimes lacking specifics but retaining a smell, feel and touch. I can only paraphrase one recollection.

'So, what makes you think I don't want to be here?' Lina would have asked Elio.

'How am I supposed to know what you want?'

She stared – no more words.

'Stop listening to your brother.'

'Let's finish this later.'

Lina would have known she had pushed too far.

Gianni's persona hid under a seemly quiet, stocky figure, confident in his speech, willing to help, but just so far. Dad spoke of Gianni's ability to ask for help or favours but offering little in return when the time came to repay the favour. He could see Mom always agreeing, always taking her brother's side in conversations. Dad had long forgiven Mom.

The 1944 film *Gaslighting* defined my uncle. He insisted that remaining in Ingham was a bad idea with few prospects and that life would be better in the city. I never knew why he changed his mind.

Gianni placed his hand on her shoulder, leaned over and whispered in her ear.

'It's time to leave this place.'

Elio hesitated, glared at Gianni, but stayed silent.

'Lina. You look tired. Maybe you're just not managing your time well here. You've always been a bit distracted, haven't you?'

'I've been trying to keep everything together,' Lina said.

'Really? Because I remember when we were back in Italy, you were always confused and needed reminding about things. I guess some things never change.'

'I don't remember it that way; anyway, I've always been pretty organised here in Ingham.' Lina replied abruptly.

'Well, it looks like your memory isn't working. You're a bit of a mess. It's not bad; it's just who you are.'

'That's not fair. You know I don't want to be here.'

'Of course. It's okay to admit it. You're human, after all.'

'I'm doing the best I can.'

'If your best isn't good enough, maybe you leave Ingham. Just admit it's not the place for you.'

'Maybe.'

Of course, I've known Gianni all of my life. I wanted him to be a significant figure in this story. The question of whether he needed to be included in the narrative was already answered years ago by his actions. If I hadn't grasped the tangled threads of his influence, the subtle pull of his words, the way he steered conversations with a well-placed sigh or a carefully timed pause, he might have faded into the background, a bit player in the main act.

His crucial historical involvement as the direct conduit between Australia and Italy meant that he needed to be there to explain why Mom was here. Is this how we want to remember history? Through the lens of my bias?

I know this view is in retrospect. It hadn't always been so. During the intervening years, he was easy to forget and ignore; he had no real impact on my life, but I needed to pay attention to his past influence on those around me.

I think I liked him once. I certainly had sympathy for him when my aunt died. I loved her. In the following years, attitudes changed, actions became more than words, and the drift to unpleasantness completed his journey. He's still alive, living with dementia. Maybe his inclusion in this story should be just a footnote, but I know it can't be.

Rosy had always been in the background, playing the necessary supporting role. Her marriage to Lino in the fifties was destined to be a formative union, and their subsequent ownership of a cane farm meant permanent settlement in far North Queensland. Lino, too, was an immigrant of the fifties, emigrating from the same area as Dad.

Rosy and Lino were to become good friends with Mom and Dad through work and social connections. It seemed destined that their life experiences paralleled each other. The obvious difference was that they called Ingham home.

Now that she had established herself as the wife of a cane farm owner, this came with certain responsibilities and duties. She was to go and find cane cutters when times were busy. Rosy was reluctant to go to the Royal Hotel alone; it was a blokey business. If Elio were available, he would go to the Hotel for her and round up whoever he could.

I wanted to write her a letter of thanks after we had visited. I wasn't sure how I would phrase it, though. I wanted to write and not call. I thought I would reference Maya Angelou, 'People will forget what you said, people will forget what you did, but people will never forget how you made them feel.' I may still write.

The Royal Hotel, established in 1886, was the place to be in Ingham. Not just another rural pub but the heartbeat of the town.

The hotel was a product of its past, constantly changing and dynamic, reflecting its purpose as a meeting hub, a place to do deals or source additional workers. It reflected the customs of its time, from drinking after work to the social meeting place or as a function venue. Money was so freely spread around that one was unsure what was legal or otherwise. Dad recollected the day when a rather scruffy cane farmer drinking at the bar, overhearing the publican complaining about life in general, made an offer then and there to buy the pub. Such were the money and energy in the cane fields in the fifties.

Every Saturday night at the Royal Hotel was a stage, and Lina never missed her cue. She moved down the stairs with practised ease in her handmade yellow and white cotton dress, the hem brushing her legs as she stepped into the room. Anticipation flickered in her eyes, the familiar thrill of knowing she would be noticed. But now, at twenty-three, it was tempered with something sharper. The glances, the murmurs, the approving nods still pleased her, but a quiet cynicism had settled in beneath it, whispering that admiration was fleeting and the night, like all the others, would end the same way.

Her eyes focused as she soaked in the present. Her feet touched the fleur-de-lis-patterned carpet, and her hands slid along the timber handrail. She had another rendezvous with Elio, and she joined him and smiled. She wasn't my mom yet.

Elio had seen something intriguingly incomplete and unsettled about her a year before. She had been in Ingham for a year and a half and had begun to change and adapt to her new environment; the snakes no longer bothered her, the heat became the norm, and her work for a dressmaker was temporarily satisfying. Relationships became all the more important.

Such was the typical Saturday night in Ingham — a place of courtship rituals, ballroom dancing and beer drinking.

There were always those who struggled with the cane fields. Some described them as invisible cages, trapping all that entered. But people did come and go. The resilient ones stayed, and others moved on to less difficult work, saddened they couldn't cope. Dad's brother, Otto, who had accompanied him, was one of those. Work was too hard, and he left for the relative safety of farm work.

Expectations were restricted to a narrow view of success, money, property, and possessions. You came from nothing, and there were only two ways to go. You could lose yourself in the addictive constant struggle to make it, or leave and find a different path.

There was a futility in thinking you could delay the inevitable. Elio had seen the end coming for some time, felt it in each season as they came and went. He had an enduring sense of place in Ingham, and was sure he could deal with the debilitating work and the constant pressure from Lina. Ultimately, they moved to Sydney in the seventh year, where they remained for the rest of their lives. Moving wasn't anyone's decision but his. He came to realise that his time had run out. His body could no longer cope, and the supply of willing workers was challenging. People already had started talking about machinery taking the place of able-bodied men. Cane cutters were finally rendered obsolete in the 1960s with mechanisation of the harvest.

They returned to Italy only once in the intervening years, and never to Ingham. The emotional disconnect between the fields and Italy seemed complete.

I wondered if this story had heroes or villains, but realised they were just a series of trajectories destined to occupy the same space and time in history. Dad continued to be as hard-working as ever. He did find his peace and home away from the fields. Mom remained a homemaker, forever surrounded by friends and relatives. Gianni's influence never left her; she was under his spell until the very end. Rosy remained a lifelong friend.

Gianni and his family also moved to Sydney. He sought out his fortune and, in many ways, succeeded, but he struck a lonely figure for the rest of his life, with few friends.

The city of Como, on the southernmost tip of Lake Como, is a little over an hour by train from Milano Centrale railway station. I arrived at San Giovanni Station late that afternoon in March, and it was good to be back.

Como was a place I ignored for years. It was on the other side of the world. Growing up, I only knew it through conversations with friends and family. I heard the stories and filed them away as interesting but nothing more.

I joined the early morning crowd the next day, standing at the counter, sipping espresso and listening to the clattering of cups and saucers. Brioches being served one after the other in many flavours, each looking delicious. My favourite, mandorla (almond), if you could get it. People leisurely strolling along lakeside paths, water lapping along the edges as ferries made their way to the next stop.

It was *primavera* (spring).

Hills plunging dramatically into the lake, the furthest with fading snows of brilliant white. Ducks gliding and diving below the water, waterfowl flapping, attempting to fly, and rows and rows of ducklings following. Much like the mudskippers of Queensland, heaving themselves across the land, grasping for every breath in humid air, taking a single step before darting back into brackish water... except Queensland has no discernible spring.

I knelt and dipped my hand into the clear water, craving its cold touch. It sharpened every sense slipping through my fingers, so contrary to the heavy heat of the place I was born.

I don't automatically love places I visit. Mostly, I just tolerate them. Ingham and the cane fields were like that. Ingham, a town desperately devoid of physical beauty, redeemable only through memories and the stories of people. But Como?

We had been invited to a function at Como Yacht Club one evening. Standing on the chilly deck, I stared into the distance across the lake. There was a moment when rolling clouds descended onto its surface in a seemingly cascading avalanche from the hills.

Light rain began to fall, and with it that unmistakable scent. Over my many visits, somewhere, somehow, Como had begun to feel like home.

People experience the world through the spirit of each place that inhabits it at a particular time, and it's okay to move on. I know Mom and Dad did. They also lived through a war and realised that the place they loved no longer held that sense of home. Devastating. I knew this place was infused with my parents' early life history, some of which I'd not uncovered, understood, or extracted from those who knew. For me, it represented a quiet form of logic. Some pieces would be lost forever, but enough would remain to preserve a sense of completeness.

It was my last day, and the weather was unusually kind. Warm. I had missed the sunrise, though it was only just climbing over the mountain peaks. The city was still bathed in shades of soft grey. Early morning has a way of stripping away the colours but bringing such clarity.

I stood on the balcony of the apartment, gripping the handrail. Tried to imagine what Dad saw and felt from his balcony in a foreign land. Empathised with Mom, transported to a land she first despised, then found, despite all the challenges, her forever home in. I was pleased about that, but sorry for the losses along the way.

And here I am, always returning to Italy, trying to recapture a time and place I just can't let go of, knowing that they did.

BIBLIOGRAPHY

Vidonya Balanzategui, Bianka & James Cook University of North Queensland. Department of History and Politics, *Gentlemen of the Flashing Blade*, (Townsville, Qld.: Dept. of History and Politics, James Cook University, 1990).

William A. Douglass, *From Italy to Ingham*, (St. Lucia, Qld.: University of Queenslands Press, 1995).

Ray Lawler, *Summer of the Seventeenth Doll: A Play in Three Acts*, (First performance 1955). https://www.youtube.com/watch?v= _2D3ioAH6_4

CAFÉ MATHEMATICS

HENRIK OBBEKAER RASMUSSEN

A CURIOUS CALL TO THE TUTOR

September 1997, student café at the Faculty of Science, University of Copenhagen

As I am leaving the café, an unknown number appears on the LCD screen of the grey Nokia 8810. The voice is that of a middle-aged man, speaking in Danish with an old-fashioned accent:

'Is this Henrik Rasmussen?'

'It is.'

'Do you teach mathematics?'

'I do.'

Then, as if offering a choice of pastry, I list the main first-year subjects: 'Linear algebra, calculus, probability theory, mechanics?'

'Let's discuss when we meet,' he says, even if I have not suggested meeting.

'What's your name?'

'This is unimportant right now,' he says.

Twelve years earlier, I had enrolled to study mathematics at an engineering school in Denmark, one mixing both Continental and

English traditions. Standard material was taught in large lecture theatres with hundreds of students, while advanced topics were consigned to small offices, where researchers would tutor, at most, a handful of committed students. The place was ugly, sixties-style concrete pre-fabs exposed to rain and wind, but the atmosphere was enthusiastic. And the parties were exuberant, often finishing next morning in a grimy canal-side bar.

A paternal uncle had persuaded me to enrol at this engineering school, to study 'applied mathematics' instead of the 'pure' sort popular at the University of Copenhagen. This uncle himself was a professor of applied mathematics, heading a department in Ontario. At my first mention of an interest in 'purity', he had bellowed: 'A waste of time! How can you tell if a pure mathematician is an extrovert? He will look at YOUR shoes instead of his own. I see them only in the afternoons, scurrying along departmental corridors.'

My father and his brothers grew up in seaside villages — 'so poor we had herring every day for breakfast' — but they excelled in school, winning them scholarships for private education. As adults, the oldest of the three brothers, also an applied mathematician of sorts, was the more formal. His manners were smooth and old-fashioned. He would wear a suit at home. But the middle brother, the Canadian, liked to provoke. He would lecture in clogs, to students wearing ties. As a conversation starter, he would pose a question: 'So what are you complaining about today?'

At some point, he bellowed: 'Certainly, don't go to Cambridge!' But I applied and they let me in. After a PhD and then a research fellowship, followed by a series of clashes with sundry authority figures, I am now dispensing lessons to first-year university students at various stages of despair.

Despite suspecting it will be a waste of time, and despite having plenty of students, I do agree to meet the caller a few days later.

METROPOLIS: THE 'MOTHER-CITY'

Spring 1934, Berlin, Kurfürstendamm

As she does every Thursday after piano, Gretel is strolling along the Kurfürstendamm. A head of black locks, almond-shaped eyes, wearing a short blue-and-white dress of silk, a trace of Guerlain trailing in the air. A Rolls-Royce cabriolet is parked in front of the Café Kranzler. Women in elegant hats are meeting for coffee and pastry, while men in tailored suits are having serious conversations about politics. Gretel's older brother Siegfried is in a wicker chair on the terrasse, underneath a modernist lamppost. A successful left-wing journalist, he is admired in some quarters and reviled in many others. From a forgotten cigarette in his mouth, ash is dropping unnoticed on the blank pages of a notebook.

'Everybody is leaving,' says Siegfried. 'It is getting too dangerous.'

'Mama and Papa say it will pass,' says Gretel. 'And leaving for where, exactly? To the dust and ruins of the Mandate? Over my dead body. Let's not rush decisions.'

At the next table, a pale man with thin lips is sipping cognac, while listening attentively. From time to time, he pats a gasping *Bulldogge*, lying in repose beneath the table. As Siegfried pays the bill, the dog waddles over to their table, where it begins to relieve itself at the lamppost, next to Siegfried's shoes, who pretends not to notice. The dog owner begins to laugh, louder and louder, going on like a wind-up toy that will not stop.

<hr />

SHARED INTERESTS

September 1997, again the student café within the Faculty of Science, University of Copenhagen

A week later, at the entrance to the café, a man asks: 'Are you Henrik Rasmussen, PhD, the maths tutor? Then I am ...'

He gives his name. Since he might still be alive, for all I know, let us call him 'S.K.' here. It is an unobtrusive name, similar to 'Peter Jones' in English. Once common, his first name now has rustic and working-class connotations. The surname is a common patronymic, suggesting a family origin in the countryside some three or four generations ago. A man of the *Volk*, surely? S.K. is wearing a navy-blue suit, a windbreaker and sneakers. He is bobbing back and forth on his feet, as if barely containing the excitement. He might be fifty or so. The build is slender, the hair dark with streaks of grey. The blue-grey eyes move quickly. 'Can we sit in the corner?'

Once more, I ask what kind of mathematics we should be studying. And, once more, he evades the question. I begin to plot my exit. However, the conversation takes an unexpected turn. Did I really do a PhD? On what exactly? He probes my knowledge of mathematics, asking questions beyond the level of a first-year student. I outline the story of John von Neumann (1903-1957), whose work I have spent years exploring.

The scion of a Jewish banking family in Budapest, von Neumann had started life as a mathematical prodigy, showing astounding powers of mental calculation and a near-photographic memory. As an adult, it is said, he memorised the Manhattan phone book, as well as works on ancient history.

Still young, von Neumann made seminal contributions to pure mathematics, sorted out the mathematical foundations of quantum mechanics, co-invented the field of game theory ('how to bet'), now central to economics. In his youth, von Neumann moved to Göttingen to work with David Hilbert, the grandfather of German (even world) mathematics. With regard to Berlin, it was one of the few places where von Neumann, as a Jew, could still find employment. But the Nuremberg Race Laws of 1935 brought an end to all that. Von Neumann prophesied that German science would take generations to recover; but it turns out he was too optimistic.

Academic brilliance got von Neumann a visa for America, where he eventually joined the Manhattan project to build a nuclear bomb. Later, he invented the architecture of the digital computer.

***

S.K. has cheered up noticeably, seeming relieved about something. He searches the leather bag. Then pulls out a worn volume of Hilbert's multi-volume *Gesammelte Werke*. I notice for the first time the vigorous tremors of his left arm.

'Ha ha! The effect of twenty years of poisoning by psychiatrists. They were supposed to cure my manic depression. But it only got worse. Now, I have to live with incurable nerve damage.'

Then he recounts the story of a professor of medicine, at the leading hospital in Copenhagen, who allegedly raped anaesthetised female patients. Once discovered, colleagues chose to hush it up: 'Why throw stones?' The professor was banished to a small hospital in the provinces. Everybody knew yet looked the other way. You probably know the psychiatrists' enthusiasm about '*Rassenhygiene*?'

Then he returns to the topic of mathematics:

'We should read Hilbert's collected works in the original. How is your German?'

***

I arrived expecting to tutor first-year — perhaps even pre-university — mathematics, but now this student wants to read foundational works, at a level where most graduate students — not least myself — will struggle. And in German. S.K. pauses, looks at the ceiling:

'My German used to be fluent. Mama would read poetry and sing *Lieder* at nighttime.'

I note that, as in French, he stresses the second syllable of 'Mama', which I believe to be old-fashioned German. Then he begins to hum a *Lied* of long ago, while swinging a trembling arm as if conducting, before reciting a poem from Goethe:

'*Über allen Gipfeln ist Ruh*'/Above all mountain tops lies peace...

I begin to appreciate the context.

A HANGING

1936, Spandau Prison, Berlin

The prison is damp and dirty. A sickly yellow light flickers in the ceiling. Metal doors bang. Shots ring out occasionally. At night, screams reverberate through the prison. Some from torture, others from nightmares. Siegfried is sharing a 3m by 2m cell with eight prisoners. Jews, communists, agitators, according to the police. They take turns sleeping on a hard bed or on the floor.

At 8 a.m., soldiers with rifles and bayonets enter the prison cell. The prisoners are handcuffed, lined up, then asked to goose-step along the corridor and down the stairs. They enter a large cell in the basement. Three judges sit at a large wooden table, case files on their side. There are no defence lawyers. Sentences are read out. Three-fold death by hanging.

With a careful hand on the shoulders, the soldiers lead the first group of prisoners into an adjacent room. Siegfried is amongst them. A mouse scurries across the floor, disturbed by the commotion. There are three gallows. 'A New Testament reference?' Siegfried wonders. At thoughts of Gretel, tears almost well. Otherwise, he is too tired to care. 'Get on with it,' he thinks. Holding their limp and bruised bodies, the guards drag foul hoods over the prisoners' heads, push them up the scaffold, then tighten the nooses.

The ground disappears beneath Siegfried's feet. A crack, and then he feels released, carried away. Opening his eyes again, he is surprised to see a forest of birch and pine. It smells of resin, fresh moss, decaying cones, and something else too. Is it almond? Flies and mosquitoes flitter between the trees. A light (or is it the Sun?) hovers in a clearing somewhere beyond. He walks towards it. 'You're early!' a friendly man shouts from the clearing. 'Move along, please.'

After five minutes, the guards pull the bodies down. One of them shines a light into Siegfried's pupils. 'This one is stone-dead.'

REMINISCENCES

December 1997, Café Europa 1989

Café Europa is my *Stammcafé* — my favourite café — in Copenhagen. The café occupies the first floor of a building in a corner of the square of Amager Torv. The existentialist philosopher Søren Kierkegaard called this square 'the navel of the world'. Beyond the narrow canal, once the landing bank for fishermen, I can see the parliament at Christiansborg Palace. The statue of Bishop Absalon, the alleged founder of Copenhagen, is covered by a thin blanket of snow. The café smells of mulled wine and cinnamon cakes. A large map covers the back wall, showing the borders of Europe at the fall of the Berlin Wall in 1989. In Viennese style, newspapers hang on bamboo sticks, for guests to read *ad libitum*.

S. K. is half an hour late. But I do not mind. I could spend my days in this café. In contrast to the well-groomed clientele, S.K. is looking dishevelled. He stutters and his left arm is trembling more than usual.

'I did not tell you much.'

'Mama did not speak for a year.'

'It was after her brother's hanging.'

'He was one of the first Jews to be murdered.'

'A critic of the regime.'

'Their father was a banker.'

'They grew up in a grand flat on the Kurfürstendamm.'

'After the war, she married a Danish aristocrat.'

'He was depressed.'

'The worst possible combination.'

'I never had a chance in this life.'

'During manic episodes, I frittered away my fortune.'

'Now, I'm living in a council flat.'

He falls silent, staring at the snowflakes falling gently on this cold and dark December day.

'But let's not linger in the past. What do you think of Cantor?'

Hilbert said of the German-Russian-Danish mathematician Cantor that he had opened up a mathematical paradise, of infinities hiding within infinities. Cantor's abstractions — then, as well as now, without any tangible applications — irked the Prussian mathematician Kronecker, a person who was well-connected and influential. He started a campaign to destroy Cantor's reputation. Cantor, who did not help his case by claiming inspiration from God, fell into depression. This depression lifted only upon the death of Kronecker. As the acerbic German-Jewish physicist Wolfgang Pauli said half a century later: 'Science progresses one funeral at a time.'

Untraceable

Slushy late-winter 1998, Café Norden, Copenhagen

We meet for the last time at the first floor of the spacious Café Norden (meaning both 'The North' or 'The Nordic Countries'), opposite the Café Europa. Its large tables of heavy planks are ideal for tutoring, with enough room for papers and books. S.K. is on much better form than last time, excited by his progress in mathematics.

'Henrik, "S.K." was not my original name. Too recognisably Jewish, I changed it.'

He tells me his birth name. Indeed, it's very recognisable. It could hardly be more so.

'They will not catch me next time. I am now untraceable.'

A few months later, on a cold and rainy day in April, I leave Denmark for good, carrying only a backpack and a single suitcase. My last memory is of the dark-grey road blending into the light-grey sky, with a sodden blackbird on the pavement. One week later, I'm installed at the Mathematical Institute of an old university, first as a visitor and then as a research associate on probation.

During the next two years, I exchange occasional emails with S.K. At some point an IT incident accidentally wipes out my contact list and I take too long to follow up. The trail goes cold.

Recently, I have searched Danish phone books, as well as registers of births and deaths. I couldn't find anybody with the name 'S.K.', of the right age and place, or with any variation of this and his birth name.

SUBMERGED IN BERLIN

Gretel remains in Berlin for the war, helped by gentile friends who provide shelter and false papers, while risking their lives. She submerges as a '*U-Boot*', a common term at the time, into gentile society. There are random controls in the streets. To avoid recognition by former classmates, who cannot all be trusted, she never goes to the Kurfürstendamm. She spends long days fearing death from bombing or from a knock on the door in a draughty chamber in a Berlin suburb. The feeling of being trapped never leaves her.

Despite Nazi efforts to make Berlin '*judenfrei*' by 1943, several thousand *U-Boote* survive in the capital. (Estimates vary a great deal.)

THE DEVIL'S MOUNTAIN

Bombings reduced the Café Kranzler, the grand apartments, and inhabitants to a mangle of bricks, splinters, and charred flesh. To rebuild the metropolis after the war, the rubble was dumped in a clearing to the West. With contributions from all Berlin, it grew into an artificial hill: *Teufelsberg* or 'Devil's Mountain'. An autumn some years ago, I visited the Teufelsberg with a local friend, then still a student, but now a 'Herr Professor Doktor'.

As we climbed the hill in moonlight, making for the perfect cliché of a Romantic-era landscape painting, bulky shadows darted through bushes on the side, rustling the leaves while snorting loudly with discontent. 'Wild boars, mostly harmless.'

I felt we had been transgressing.

NOTE

Scenes before and during the war are fictional. The rest are essentially non-fictional, reconstructed from memory.

Camera Obscura

Jan Fuscoe

Dad, Franco Giuseppe Oswaldo, died in 2014. He lived for 32,963 days. Born in east London, in 1923, to Italian immigrant parents — Domenico and Elvira — he was the youngest son of ten children. I never met either of my Italian grandparents.

Mum, Mary Brigid, came to England in 1948 from Leitrim in Ireland, when she was seventeen, as one of the first trainee nurses for the NHS. My Irish grandparents moved to South Wales when one of my uncles, Tom, found work down the pits. Bedwas Colliery closed in 1985, after the Miners' Strike.

Mum and Dad met at Whipps Cross hospital. Dad was working in the Pathology Lab and joked that Mum would urge her patients to produce more 'samples' so that she had an excuse to come and see him in the lab.

They worked for the NHS all their lives. It took care of them when they were sick, until Dad got dementia, when Mum looked after him at home.

By the time Mum needed round-the-clock care, 'social care' was on its knees. Mum's care home cost £6,000 a month. Then Covid came.

Mum lived for 32,957 days, just five days short of Dad's lifespan.

APRIL 2023

I'm disappearing. The photo on my travelcard seems to be 'undeveloping'. White spaces have appeared where once there was me. There's no hair on the left side of my head. I seem to be wearing a white hairpiece that hangs from a white hairband that has also suddenly appeared.

My left eye, the left side of my nose, and half my mouth is missing. My right eye looks ghoulish, as if I'm wearing a Zombie contact lens. Below my right ear, a white patch resembles a big dangly white earring.

It's probably because I keep my travelcard in my pocket, with my keys. But then, as I'm waiting for test results, it's quite possible that I *might* disappear.

I'm not sure why Dad brought my younger sister, Kay, and I into his laboratory that day. I was maybe five or six years old. Perhaps Mum was working but, looking back, she was probably with 'Peg', her younger sister, Margaret, who was sick.

I remember asking, 'Why are you crying, Mum?' when we were at Granny and Grandad's in Wales. I was sitting beside the still warm embers of an earthy peat fire that had been banked up the night before, and Mum was on the sofa facing me.

'I sat on a knitting needle,' she said. Even then, I knew that wasn't true, but I was five, or maybe six. Now I realise that Peg was dying.

Dad looked different in his white lab coat. I don't know why he wanted to take a blood sample, but I remember him gently sliding the needle into my arm and being surprised that it didn't hurt, but I did wonder why he needed so much blood. Later he told me I was A+.

The lab smelt weird. Chemically. An old photo reminds me that it was a big space with lots of desks and chairs, and stuck to the glossy cream walls, with yellowing crinkled Sellotape, were dozens of pieces of type-written paper. Shiny lino flooring looked even shinier under fluorescent lights overhead. The desks were covered in grey and black machines, with lots of knobs and dials. On the long wooden bench that stretched along one wall there were more machines, and the microscopes.

He showed me petri dishes covered in something called 'agar' that encouraged cells to grow. He sterilised a thin metal loop over a Bunsen burner, then streaked something, or nothing, across pus-coloured jelly. He might have said, 'This is where the magic happens.'

I hopped up onto the red swivel chair at the bench and shuffled up to the microscope. He slid the petri dish under the lens and told me to look through the eyepiece. 'Can you see something moving?'

Vaguely, perhaps, a squiggle, like crochet, or a fat pinky-purplish centipede. But I preferred the John Bull printing set in the side office. Using a pair of plastic tweezers, I placed tiny rubber letters into a wooden frame, pressed the frame on an ink pad, and then onto a white piece of paper to see the words appear. That *would* have been magic, but I should have placed the letters in reverse order because they appeared as non-words and made no sense.

There was a darkroom at the Path Lab. Perhaps that's when Dad became interested in photography and developing his own pictures. Always focussed, developing ideas, doing experiments, writing scientific papers.

Camera obscura (dark room) is the name for a forerunner of the early camera.

Funnily enough, our surname, Fusco, seems to come from the Latin *fuscare* 'to darken'. 'Obfuscate' comes from the same root, meaning to render 'indistinct, or unclear'.

The definition of 'Clearing':
    A dell, or a glade (noun).
    An open space, a gap, something missing, no longer there (noun).
    To free yourself from something that encumbers you or to make space to cultivate or grow (verb).
    I once found Marie Kondo's *The Life Changing Magic of Tidying Up* on a bus. I picked it up and got to work. I folded socks, stacked shirts, threw out old T-shirts, and wondered how much joy was still sparked from a dress that hadn't fitted me since 1980. Then I reached Kondo's chapter on books:

    'I now keep my volume of books to thirty at one time.'

    Clearly ridiculous. I stopped reading and left the book on the bus for someone else.

MAY 2023

I've just had a second biopsy at Bart's.
    My right breast, displayed on two screens, looked like a partial view of the Earth from space, where the sea is black, and the land is white. The consultant points out a small white island, more pixelated than the rest. It could be calcification, but it might be something else. She needs to take another look.
    As I wandered back through Smithfield's Meat Market, I could almost taste the sour scent of raw flesh. During the day, heavy, opaque, plastic curtains, reminiscent of a CSI crime scene, hide different bloody dramas, but years ago, on my way home from a club, I walked this same route in the early hours, and glimpsed carcasses hanging, dangling,

swinging, from meat hooks. No longer cow or pig. No skin, head, or hooves, just a mass of pink and white marbled meat ready to be butchered. I remember that the expression, 'Let's have a butchers' comes from the Cockney rhyming slang. 'Butcher's hook' means 'look'.

I thought of Mum bringing me a bowl of tomato soup, and Marmite on toast, whenever I was sick in bed. And of her carrying me upstairs to bed after a party. She thought I'd fallen asleep, but I remembered the feel of her arms around me.

This time last year, I was at my childhood home waiting for the clearance people.

I remember the ritual Christmas photo. Dad would set up the tripod, check the light meter, set the timer, rush back to the table — usually dressed with a red linen tablecloth, a holly and berry centre-piece, wine, laden with food — and then we'd wait. Nothing. No flash.

He'd go back to the camera but, invariably, before he got there, Flash! He'd reset the timer, rush back. Nothing. And repeat. Never failed to get a laugh. Over the years the cameras got smaller, so no need for a light meter, and with an automatic flash the process was much quicker, just not as funny.

Over the years Dad changed cameras — Polaroid, Pentax, Canons, SLRs, Nikons, digital, camcorders — and he upgraded his editing equipment too, from a splicing machine, where he'd cut the film and 'Sellotape' it back together on the dining table, to a full editing suite set up in one of the now spare bedrooms at the family home.

Dad was often behind a camera.

Now, watching back family DVDs — birthdays, playing in the garden or in the park, with Judy, our beloved corgi (who could run up the steps of the slide with us, before sliding down to the bottom), weddings, grandchildren, as they arrived — I remembered that we were sometimes irritated by Dad's directorial directions from behind the camera:

'Say something, Jan,' 'Look at me, Jan' (or Marian, Susan, Kay, Mum). But I'd forgotten how funny he was, and I could hear the love in his voice, and remembered his constant focus on us from a place where he felt so comfortable, behind a lens.

JUNE 2023

I took a different route today. I got off near the Barbican and see/don't see the bank where I used to work when I was in my twenties. I reflect that every building I've ever worked in has disappeared. No refurbishment, just torn down, cleared, replaced.

I cut through to Smithfield's again and see/don't see the little Italian café. And there/where is the bar with the neon sign that I liked? Gone. Is that another sign?

My planet Earth is on screen again. More white islands than there should be.

The nurses, radiologists, oncologists tell me their names and job titles, but I rarely remember them. I try to focus on what they're telling me:

'Another biopsy.' 'Two more biopsies.'

But I remember Julianna. Beautiful, black, and confidently reassuring.

'We just need to get a better picture.'

Another young, pretty nurse, with perfect TV-advert teeth, asks 'What are you going to do after this?' as she sandwiches my breast between two plastic trays.

I'm scared, afraid they've forgotten the pain relief.

'Don't worry. I'll give you plenty of the good juice,' Julianna laughed.

Lidocaine is *definitely* magic. A slight scratch, then nothing. Total numbness.

The machine whirrs quietly, like a faint electric typewriter. The nurse distracts me again, asking 'What are you going to have for dinner?'

I feel the sensation of pulling, and pushing, but no pain.

'Have you got any holidays planned?'

I might have been at the hairdressers, and wished I was.

We had a galley kitchen that backed onto the living room where we watched telly, in black-and-white. Sometimes, when I slid the kitchen door back, it was in darkness, like a magician's cave. 'Quick, close the door,' he'd say. A red light glowed somewhere and, lined up along the worktop, there was an enlarger, and three shallow trays filled with fluid. I remember the smells. Not acrid exactly, but particular, pungent, metallic.

I watched Dad cut the negative from a reel of film and slot it into the top part of the enlarger. Then he took a piece of white photographic paper from a bright chromium-yellow Kodak box and placed it at the bottom of the enlarger. He told me that the light would project an image onto the paper below, yet it was still blank.

Using wooden tongs or plastic tweezers, I can't remember, he slid the paper, with a faint plash, into the first tray. Developer[1] has a sweetish metallic smell.

I wish I'd paid more attention at school. Chemistry is magic. As he moved it back and forth, gently pressing it under the fluid, the white paper became grainy. Patches of light-grey, grey, grey-black, and black slowly appeared in places. Something was being revealed. A face, a space, faces in spaces. I think of my 'white islands' on screen at the hospital. What might they be developing into?

---

1. Developing agents are metol (monomethyl-p-aminophenol hemisulfate), phenidone (1-phenyl-3-pyrazolidinone), dimezone (4,4-dimethyl-1-phenylpyrazolidin-3-one), and hydroquinone (benzene-1,4-diol). Alkaline agent such as sodium carbonate, borax, or sodium hydroxide to create the appropriately high pH.

Once he was happy with it, he lifted the paper out and slid it into the second tray to stop the development. 'Stopper' smells of vinegar[2], still a favourite smell. Happy memories of cold, vinegared chips from the 'fish and chip' dinner Dad bought after picking Mum up from a late shift. There were always some left for us in the morning. Only Kay and I seemed to be fans of already salted and vinegared chips, with a thin scraping of Marmite added, reheated under the grill.

A bit more swishing, then the last tray. The worst. 'Fixer'[3] smells like rotten eggs.

Final swoosh, then he pegged the paper up on a line he'd fashioned in the tiny kitchen where Mum had made dinner a couple of hours earlier. Was she irritated that he'd taken over her space? I can't remember. I expect she said, 'Don't forget to clear up after yourself.'

I never gave it much thought back then. Didn't all dads do this?

JULY 2023

A vacuum excision sounds banally domestic. I imagined Julianna 'hoovering' around for more cells, some of which would land up on a slide under a microscope.

The surgeon is talking me through the results. I can't focus. She's young, bright-eyed, and smiley, but her words make no sense. They're jumbling around in my head, but some are clearer, louder, like foghorns.

'Mastectomy.' 'Double mastectomy.' 'Braca.'[4]

'What do you think?' she asks.

2. A 2% dilution of acetic acid.
3. Sodium thiosulfate (sodium hyposulfite), $Na_2S_2O_3$, dissolves the part of the silver salts coated onto film which remain unchanged by exposure to light.
4. Mutation of the BReast CAncer gene significantly increases the chances of developing breast cancer.

I *can't* think. I'm numb, but know salty tears are running down my face.

'Could I chat to your sister? To get a better picture?'

She squiggles down unintelligible words then hands back my phone.

She carries on talking, but I only pick up:

'... seems your sister wasn't tested for Braca...'

'... she probably doesn't have Braca...'

'... you probably don't have Braca...'

'... much smaller operation...'

'... excision of small duct...'

'We'll keep an eye on it.'

House clearance is something no-one warns you about.

It was a bright, sunny day when three strangers came to clear the house where my parents had lived for sixty years. I couldn't watch, so I sat in the garden with my dog, Ginger, who, oblivious to the drama unfolding behind me, ran round and round the garden, as all our childhood dogs had done before her.

I didn't see, but I could hear... the crash, smash, crash of breaking glass and crockery. Were they just sweeping everything out of the kitchen cupboards onto the floor? I couldn't look, but I could tell that the clearers had moved into the downstairs utility room, where the gardening stuff was kept.

I kept some of Dad's tools, and the gloves and boots that Mum wore for gardening, and a lifetime of Dad's photos, slides, and negatives.

More smashing and crashing. Were those Dad's dozens of brown glass jars, now? The ones with cork stoppers and faded labels with words like 'Acetic Acid', 'Citric acid', 'Sodium' something or other?

Only now I remember what the jars were for, he used them to create photographic magic.

'There's too much to take,' the clearers tell me. They'll have to come back tomorrow. After they leave, I vacuum the rooms they've cleared. There's a sheet in the middle of the front room covered in stuff they've taken from the cupboards — his books, opera CDs, libretti — all just thrown in a pile. I see more Kodak boxes and must look through them again. They're full of photos that never made it into any album — of the garden when the swing was still up, Mum standing in the snow, and a raggedy photo of Dad as a small boy.

How had I missed that one? Another of Dad in army uniform. I knew that he served in the medical corps in Vienna during WWII. Apparently, they didn't want him for active service, being of Italian origin. I remember him telling me that his dad, the *nonno* I never met, would have been interned as an enemy alien, had he lived. And there's Mum's little blue hairbrush. I put it in my bag, with more photos, and cuttings of Mum's jasmine and honeysuckle, and a garden gnome with a chipped hat. So much, too much, and not enough.

I found the microscope at the bottom of their wardrobe, along with some old cameras. I didn't know that he had his own microscope. I couldn't see it thrown out, but what was I going to do with a microscope?

The shiny mahogany box has been sitting, unopened, on my sideboard for more than a year. It's heavy, over a foot tall, with a folding brass carry handle at the top that is as tarnished as the key at the front that opens the hinged door. Inside is a 'Discovery' microscope, with the manufacturers' name, J. SWIFT & SON LONDON, engraved on the horseshoe-shaped base.

J. Swift & Son was a London laboratory instrument manufacturer, established in 1857. The Discovery was a portable microscope designed specifically for Captain Scott's 1901-1904 *RRS Discovery* expedition to carry out scientific research in the Antarctic. It features a stage large enough to hold a petri dish.

A year later, and I wonder what I'll do with it all: the piles of stamps I used to collect, the small hand-written tags Dad had made for his files: 'Poetry', 'Dog', 'Genealogy', a separate file for each of his children, old schoolbooks.

I could clear out some of these, surely? My old science books, full of Bunsen burners, distillation with a Liebig condenser, hand-drawn pictures of cells, and the results of experiments:

'Magnesium metal: A silver piece of metal. The metal set alight and then broke. The change was permanent.'

My writing changed. Once confident, written with different coloured felt-tipped pens, accompanied by neatly drawn pictures and diagrams. Once I moved to a new school my writing hardly rose above the line. Barely legible. My writing had almost disappeared, as I felt I had.

I thought about 'Discards', an essay written by Nicholson Baker for the *New Yorker* in 1994. It railed against the predilection of libraries to destroy their hard copies, specifically library index cards, in favour of digitalisation. Baker wondered how much was lost when numbers and letters were accidentally mis-transposed, and mused on the loss of the individuals who were once instantly recognisable (to those who knew them) by the type of pen they used, the colour of the ink they used, and the slope and curve of their letters.

I remember the weekly trips to the library with Dad, watching the librarian, usually a woman, riffling through little rust-red or dove-blue envelopes, held in a heavy wooden drawer. The firm ink 'stamp' of the return date. I thought, 'I'd like to do that when I grow up.'

I'd cut the corners off dozens of postcards that had arrived, for Dad, from all over the world, from America to Zimbabwe. I wanted the beautiful stamps.

I find the postcards, with the stamp-less corners carefully Sellotaped back on, and notice, perhaps for the first time, that each comes from a university or medical laboratory, requesting copies of

Dad's scientific articles: 'The role of extracellular slime secretion in the swarming of Proteus', 'A dual composite medium for the differentiation of the pathogenic enterobacteria and coliform organisms', 'A multiple-inoculation urea plane medium', 'Two prototype safety pipetting devices'.

---

14 August 2023

Operation Day:

My surgeon tells me she'll carry out the operation at the Nuffield Centre, close by. The elegant woman who walks us over wears a neat black dress, expensive-looking shoes with low Cuban heels, and beautiful gold earrings that we both comment on. Beyond the smart reception desk, I wait in an area full of brightly coloured club chairs and soothing wall art. There's a coffee machine.

I'm shown to my private room, complete with white waffle robe, slippers, and a TV, and then a procession of nurses and anaesthetists ask questions: 'Are you allergic to anything?', 'Do you have diabetes?' before taking my blood pressure and administering the pre-op anaesthetic.

Hours later I wake up, pain-free, and order lunch from a menu. I have the soup. There's no Marmite on toast option.

Pathologists are like detectives, using a microscope to observe things that can't be seen with the naked eye. I learn that they distinguish normal cells from cancer cells by studying the shape and size of the nucleus. After being stained with dye, cancer cells appear darker than normal cells.

That's part of what Dad did, in his white lab coat — tested and analysed samples, looked through microscopes, focussed on blood cells and tissue, looking for subtle differences in colour or shape. Had he diagnosed breast cancer?

I kept Dad's collection of coins that, as a child, I painstakingly sorted by value and year. The little pots that I kept still have my yellow heart-shaped stickers on them with childish, but carefully handwritten classifications, like '3d 1963', or '1d 1872'.

In among the pots, full of halfpennies, pennies, and threepenny bits, I found a single microscope slide. A magenta-pink splodge, the size and shape of a molar. A tiny label, handwritten, in ink, tells me

'Liver r. Gall Bladder.' It's not Dad's writing.

I read somewhere that breast cancer cells are pink. My favourite colour. And remembered that 'thrupenny (bit)' is cockney rhyming slang for 'tit'.

Post-op, my surgeon tells me that everything went well, but one of my many (nine and counting) biopsies showed evidence of cancerous cells. Another operation.

As I unlocked it, I realised that the last person to touch the microscope was probably Dad.

Several brass tubes, the size and shape of shotgun cartridges, are held in the door, with another three lenses to the side of the microscope. These are the lenses that screwed into the carousel above the stage.

The initials 'I.M.S' are engraved onto the neck of the microscope. Who, or what, was IMS? A faint hand-written 'Swa' is just visible on the side of the carrying case. Was it part of a surname? How did Dad come by it?

I slid the slide onto the stage. There were no clips to hold it in place. This was a Discovery, after all, and the stage was made for large petri dishes, not slides.

I found a bulb for the electric light and switched it on. I peered into the eyepiece. It was black and blurry.

There were three lenses on the carousel. I moved them around, trying to focus. Nothing.

I twiddled the adjustment knobs that brought the stage closer to the lens. Nothing.

I had no idea how to use a microscope. I switched the light off and put it away.

---

11 September 2023

Operation 'Lymph Nodes'

This time a 'tracer' dye will be injected into the area recently operated on. The Isosulfan Blue dye will stain the lymph nodes that are reached first, helping the surgeon locate the right area to biopsy.

I wait outside the Nuclear Medicine department for what seems like an age, long enough for me to Google 'Nuclear Medicine' and discover that the dye is radioactive. Should I be concerned? There is no-one around to ask. I'm not sure I'm in the right place.

Eventually someone, I'm not sure who, arrives and leads me into a huge room dominated by an enormous scanner, and I wait again. The nurse, radiologist, or radiographer, I'm not sure who, explains the procedure. Perhaps she's forgotten, or doesn't know, about my operation (though the scar is still vivid), but, without an anaesthetic, she jabs a long, curved needle into my nipple and starts to push. I cry out with the pain. She's sorry, but it's too late to anaesthetise the area now, so she carries on.

The day is a blur, but I remember walking along a maze of winding corridors with hastily stuck-up signs directing us ahead, then right, or left, then right, until I eventually arrive in a ward with four beds where I'm to wait, the only patient there. The experience couldn't be more different. No soothing wall art here. No coffee machine or smartly dressed staff. I get under an NHS-issue cellular blue blanket and fall asleep.

My surgeon wakes me to tell me that, thanks to a more complicated case being referred back to the NHS, I can be operated on again at the Nuffield Centre. I'm pleased, of course, but wonder how many 'more complicated' cases come back to the NHS?

I found an article Dad had written when he was nearly eighty years old: 'Stereopsis and the role of the Spherical Retinae.'

He conducted an experiment that involved the construction of a square plywood box with a hole providing a close fit for lens tubes in line with the camera lens, and a 60-watt matte lightbulb ('the print on the bulb removed with a cream cleaner', he'd written). He mounted a 'bi-convex lens of about 65mm focal length in the lid of a 35mm film (black) cassette case, and an opaque plastic iris with a 10mm hole was affixed to the outside of the lens, giving an aperture of about f6.5'. I have no idea what he hoped to show — surely something about how the eye can focus and send its message to the brain — but I couldn't make sense of it, and it served to remind me again how much more than 'Dad' he was.

OCTOBER 2023

I went to a friend's art class. It was a revelation. First the brilliant bubble-gum colours of the watercolour inks — hyacinth blue, olive green, chromium yellow, magenta pink. Such innocent colours, now tinged with drama. The thick, expensive paper absorbed every brushstroke, or drop, of watercolour ink, which dried with a pleasing sharp border that was a shade or two darker. We learned how to build the colours, and shapes, with every layer adding contrast and texture, but always being able to see what lay beneath.

'When you stop focussing, the magic happens,' the artist told us.

Maybe.

I have my last appointment on December 11th. Dad's birthday.

Today I've been alive for 22,738 days.

RIVER

CHRIS HAYWARD

'Time is a river which sweeps me along, but I am the river.'[1]

I ts sources surface in ditches and fields beyond the small town of Debenham and its waters blend with the sea over the wide shingle barred estuary at Felixstowe Ferry. Suffolk's River Deben is about twenty-five miles long — a river which has enchanted me all the years I have lived here. Although there is no linear river path, it's possible to walk its length via circuitous routes and ancient footways.

In between these paths, I know there are creeks and marshes, forests and farmland, secret and inaccessible places, all retaining isolation and mystery alongside those open views of water and Suffolk skies. The connection with these quiet waters mirrors much of my internal world, often undisclosed, even to myself. Writers, filmmakers, painters and poets have been inspired by it. History has marked it. Industry has churned it. I plan to walk it.

I haven't mapped this walk myself. I've found a handy little

---

1. Jorge Luis Borges, *Labyrinths,* (Penguin Classics, 2000), P269.

book by Nick Cottam[2] who very kindly describes ten journeys which will take me from beginning to end. Two stalwart friends, Trudi and Ann, have agreed to be with me when they can. The three of us have done a few quests before, so, let's look on this as another one.

SPRING

Trudi and I did the first walk in late April on a cool morning when the grey brightness promised breaking sun. I had left Dave at home. He talked about losing heart, making little progress, not able to take more than a few small steps before he got breathless. There was a gloom about his situation — one he had to live in, manage, face... whatever the right phrases are when someone has a hard and unknown condition. Although I could not share his dark room, I wanted to be at its door. We were dependent on the results of his scan to know where that door might lead and what the room would hold.

Earlier, he had shared his thoughts with me, as I read his notebook.

'April 2022
I want to get through the day at my pace. Breathlessness intensifies when I get out of the car. Need to rest to normalise my breathing. What next? Always looking for rest... I think about all the little impediments to normal life, eternal, internal restlessness from knowing that this is not me and the life I want to live, but I remain trapped and beaten down; the terrible frame of mind I have entered, where I have stopped thinking and feeling in a measured and constructive way and instead, simply feeling "done to". What choice is there for Chris and me? If it's about getting through the day at my

---

2. Nick Cottam, *Walking the Deben: Ten walks from source to mouth*, (UK: LoTD Publishing, 2020).

pace, I need to make the space just to get by. Use that space for deep breathing, for simple tasks. And try to regain and retain my dignity.'

I realised that day — well, I always knew, as did he — that separating myself from a difficult situation is the way I deal with a lot of hard things. I know I have the facility to focus almost entirely on the task in hand. It's a very helpful resource in terms of getting jobs done, but also in avoiding painful issues; by not being in them, they are not real, are they? The walking fulfils this need to be in a different place, with different people, involved in different lives. I don't have to be in my own for a while.

In the wild grasses of St Mary of Grace churchyard, Trudi and I sit for a while in easy companionship, delighted to discover the flimsiest of wild strawberry leaves nestling amongst the blades. We have already lost ourselves in the apple tree acres of the Aspall estate, untamed blossom filling our skyscape. Petals from St Mary's margins escape the wall and litter the roadside. That sense of exuberant abundance is all around us. I have a burst of excitement and optimism that good omens are blooming alongside primroses and cowslips. Their juxtaposition of delicate and robust mirrors how I feel about myself.

We find Stone Street, a ravine of a road with high banks on either side. The path rises onto these banks and we look down into the gravelly dip. Here, the street is also the river, a swollen ford when the rain beats and the river's high. Today there's naught but a central trickle. Somewhere about is the Groaning Stone which, I'm told, turns and moans at the full moon's midnight hour. I forget to look.

It's May, and Trudi and I meet at The Queen in Brandeston. As we cross a slabbed concrete bridge to walk through buttercup meadows, the Deben here is still a rivulet. Undulating fields rise above the road and where the track is punctuated by grand oaks, I can turn to broad views across the valley, towards open swathes, greening hedgerows. Stopping for snacks, it is nettley, scented by dampened grass. We are peaceable and recalibrating. By the river bank the invasive Himalayan Balsam is extending its ground. Always something which shouldn't be there. Here, the Deben is a definite stream — it looks like a proper water course. Cottam tells us these river stretches might give us the flash of a kingfisher but we're not lucky today. The flow sounds stronger. Perhaps the water is singing. Or is it the wind chiming through the confetti leaves of alders and poplars?

I have described Trudi as a stalwart friend. By that I mean loyal and reliable. I admire the way she tells me about the things she is afraid of. She speaks as an artist who is painting colour into her life after many years of being bound in monochrome. On our walk, she reflects about her children. One is spiralling into another failed endeavour and two are fulfilling their talents in writing and art. She is well able to talk about them and the ins and outs of her concerns and I encourage her to do so. About my own life, I am more circumspect but when she asks, she listens too. I am able to describe the tingling around my shoulders and chest, the anxiety lump as I swallow.

There are buttercup meadows on this walk; just look at their shining spread! Leaving their golden faces, we rise from the valley to the windy rises of the field edge where the spring wheat shivers. Then down again and across water meadows (no cattle, thank goodness!) to a wooden bridge where, at last, the Deben has grown up. It emerges from between willow banks into a gathering pool, deep and satisfying, surfaced with the leaf plates of water lilies. There's clear evidence of progression here as the water course widens and grows stronger. If the river can do it from such a meagre starting point, perhaps it's an allegory for progress at home, too.

Dave had the scan in early May. Dr M's subsequent letter to Dave's GP contained the stark information that: 'Given the cardiac MRI scan has revealed appearances with cardiac amyloidosis, I would recommend that he be referred to the National Amyloidosis Centre, The Royal Free Hospital in London.' We had to look up what amyloidosis was.

'May 2022
Yesterday's news has now sunk in. I have been to the website for the
Royal Free and now I feel I know a lot more about what's involved.
And I'm feeling really, really fed up... Most of all, I'm fed up with
preparing those I know and care for, for yet another round of them
having to care for me. And I really don't like the sound of the treat-
ments: chemotherapy, radiotherapy. And I'm not sure I want the
dubious honour of having a rare heart condition.
Having said all that, I hope that at the end of it all (!) I may have a
heart that functions better than it has done on occasions in the past.
Maybe that's the thing I need to focus on.'

But it's not quite as synchronised as that. Two and a half weeks have
passed since the letter arrived. When I go home, Dave tells me that
Dr M. has not yet made the referral to the Royal Free. We are both
devastated. It feels that crucial time has been lost. Recording today's
walk in my loose-leaf diary, the pages get all mixed up.

LATE SPRING

Dave and I are in the Pears building — the very swish hotel attached
to London's Royal Free Hospital. There are views across the
rooftops towards Hampstead Heath and, after Dr M. made the
referral, the hospital responded very speedily and we're on the last
day of a week of tests at the National Amyloidosis Centre. I think
Dave's being brilliant, but I know he feels on his own in a lonely
place. I want to weep but I won't. Yesterday, we made the most of
this enforced London stay with a wheelchair to get around: the
supermarket across the road, busy pavements, the George pub for
the taste of a London pint — being part of the cacophony of
normality. Today I am sitting in the corner of a scan room. Dave is
in a huge white machine. Quiet humming. Stillness. Coolness. I'm

there because when the nurses tried it previously, Dave had a panic attack.

Later, we see Dr R. who gives us the results of all the tests and options for the future. We learn that amyloidosis is a category of conditions where a set of proteins misfold into hard spikey forms and join together, causing organs to malfunction. For Dave, it appears to be affecting the heart. His heart muscle has stiffened, becoming less elastic and therefore not able to fill and pump and drain effectively. This is what is causing fatigue, breathlessness and what Dr R. calls general crappiness. There is no cure for his version: ATTR Amyloidosis. The best option is to stabilise and manage. Dr R. will put him forward for a clinical trial. Dr R. says the prognosis is two to two and a half years with a fair wind.

June 10th 2022
Good:
range of tests done;
movement better than I would have predicted.

Not good:
swollen ankles, hard tummy;
movement a bit erratic.
I can feel quite woozy at times; panic attack ended the scan early.
I have ATTR amyloidosis. I have been invited, and agreed to join, a drugs programme.
Lots I can do myself: exercise, diet, weights. My target is to walk 6 minutes non-stop.'

I'm home again and Ann, Trudi and I are walking round Ufford and Rendlesham, criss-crossing the Deben and passing over centuries of seemingly unchanged countryside. The day threatened a north wind and showers, but it's remained fine and warm. Before we reach St Gregory's church, we pass a vast archaeological site, gridded with red and yellow flags. It's here that Anglo-Saxon arte-facts have been found, along with evidence of major buildings: a royal residence from where it's believed King Raedwald ruled a major part of the East Anglian kingdom. The Deben valley, so gentle, so peaceful, yet a place of industry and turmoil.

I'm interested in history, but today I just mark the passing. I can't really remember anything about the meadows or grassy banks or what the Deben looked like. I haven't written anything about this walk in my diary, just the bit about the flags. How many six minutes did we do?

SUMMER

The tidal reach of the Deben touches Wilford Bridge, just upriver from Woodbridge. On this mid-June day, the tide is out, as the three of us walk seawards, from Woodbridge towards Kyson Point. Near the bank where the mudflats are exposed, an oystercatcher's powerful orange-red bill is relentless in the search for shellfish. Around it, the lumps of bladderwrack, the uncovered spits and channels are waiting to be protected again. Without warning, the bird rises, its piping call seeping across sea purslane and cordgrass. Two mute swans glide into sight, their wings arched in warning. A black-headed gull keeps its distance as the oystercatcher sweeps back onto the salt marsh.

We reach the Long Shed. Built as part of a complex to replace the old Whisstocks Boatyard, it's now the workshop for recreating the Anglo-Saxon ship which was unearthed by Basil Brown at Sutton Hoo in 1939. Using the abilities of skilled shipwrights and volunteers, the aim is to build a replica of the burial ship using, as far as possible, Anglo-Saxon methods.

As a talented carver, it's Dave's job to make trenails[3]. First, with the malleable green willow, he makes the blank. This is a larger version of the finished trenail and over ensuing months, will shrink as the willow dries out. He can then shape it exactly to fit its place in the ship. He's practised this many times. The frustrations of inaccu-

---

3. A trenail is a wooden nail for fastening timbers together.

racies, splitting, size faults, means it takes him about four hours to fashion one perfect trenail, but he will get quicker. Dave loves patient working with drawknife for shaping, whittling knife for precision.

When he and the Shipwright are satisfied, Dave hammers the trenail into its augured hole before forcing an exact fit by cleaving the shank with an oak wedge. Together, the hard and soft wood mean strength. After rounding and smoothing, he coats it with pine tar. Each of these trenails will help hold the mighty boat together. Eventually it will be launched on the Deben and rowed by forty oarsmen down the river to the sea and beyond, to the Thames, the Humber. Although he is no sailor, Dave would like to be part of that triumph.

Ann suggests that we go and have a look at how the ship is progressing. She is finely tuned to emotional nuances in others, never pushing forward her views, just gently suggesting something which is already in my mind. One of Dave's trenails is part of the visitor display. He's written his initials on the base. He's not here today, though I know he will be pleased that we called in. I have a moment's stillness amidst the hammering and cleaving and I want to think there is a shift in the air, a nod from the past.

After leaving the Longshed, Ann, Trudi and I resume our walk past the houseboats, accompanied by the damp smell of weed clinging to their hulls. Diverging from the path, we climb the hill to Broomheath and sit on a bench overlooking the river to the far bank. It's a painter's view across the water to Martlesham Creek and St Mary the Virgin Church, built on a bluff above the Deben and part of an ancient settlement. We've left the chill of the river wind, and the sun now warms us in these sheltered moments.

Onwards, making our way back to Woodbridge, we enter the mystery of Porter's Wood where we've been told some film makers have built an Anglo-Saxon hut. Wood and thatch. Just there in the forest. Fingers of the past touching our faces. Someone else has built a gateway out of logs. Whichever way you go through it, it leads nowhere except to the other side. I think it's a magic door but I'm not casting the right spell.

As June moves over the summer equinox, Dave moves into hospital. His feet, legs and stomach are full of fluid, and he's asked to go into hospital to have it drained. We understand that this will be about comfort, not cure. There is a lot of talking between us and there are a lot of quiet moments too. Small things matter, the sudden breathlessness, the panic attack and then the calming. It's hard to know where we'll be in a few months' time. I take his car to be cleaned, inside and out. This morning, he says he can put on his slippers more easily. We are due to go away for a big family gathering next week in Herefordshire.

June 23rd 2022
Meeting with Dr S.
-priority is getting the fluid out;
-balance needed between low blood pressure and clearing out the fluid;
-he thinks I'll be in hospital till the weekend;
-uncertain that would be OK for me to travel;
-pulled a face when I suggested I needed a holiday.'

In the end, Dave and I agreed that I shall still go to Herefordshire as we are hosting the event and Dave's sister, L, will come to stay in our home. So that someone close can visit him and do all the stuff that people in hospital need.

'30th June 2022
Pointers to progress:
-movement around the ward feels much easier;
-consultant has agreed I can take some corridor exercise;
-nurse has just confirmed I have shed 2 litres more than I ingested today;
-consultant reckons I should be ready to go home in 4-5 days.
Don't see the events of today — L taking over from Chris — as

anything other than practical significance. Nothing deep or meaning-
ful, just attempts at continuity with change of personnel. Tomorrow it
will look different.'

I leave on 1st July, due back on the 3rd.

'1st July 2022
Another weird night's sleep. 6.15am — good shave and wash (what
<u>does</u> everybody else do?!) — busy, busy ward: blood, blood pressure,
breakfast, fresh bed — can't get Sky Sports so no watching the first few
Test Match overs.
Saw Dr M. who prescribed another white bomber to really get rid of
the fluid. Also showed Chris' notes to Dr M. He was interested but
wants original correspondence i.e., he wants Dr R. to write to him
direct. He'll take notice of that.'

This is Dave's last entry. He died at ten past two in the morning of
Monday 4th July. The tipping point was reached — maybe the
kidneys, the heart, the lungs — in the end, the balance couldn't be
retrieved. The machines were one by one, over quiet time, so kindly
switched off. The bleeping was exchanged for silence. I was there,
with his daughters and his sister. Our hands were with him and each
other as he died. So peacefully. Looking like Dave. And for the first
time, I could understand that euphemism of passing away.

Perhaps it seems that this was so very sudden, but it felt to all of
us, possibly even Dave, that this was like the ebb and flow of the
tide, just an acceptance of something inevitable which couldn't be
held back. And that Dave had chosen to be the person he wanted to
be, not become the person he wasn't.

Of course, my stalwart friends came to his funeral. As I look
back now, I think he would have been proud of how it went. It
honoured and celebrated him, mourned him and then surrendered
him to the flames. Although he will not be part of the completed
Anglo-Saxon ship sailing down the river, the humour was not lost

on us all that the coincidental style of cardboard coffin that held his final journey was called 'The Deben'.

AUTUMN

This day is bright and sunny. Ann, Trudi and I are walking at Martlesham Creek. It's one of the eight creeks on this river. We cross the winter wheat fields to the water. Here are solitary little egrets and sieges of black-tailed godwits, picking and poking. Wooded banks hold slender, shifting trees, glimpses of sky, as branches wave. A great tit whistles sharply and I realise I haven't really listened to its call before. Two men are counting the godwits.

From the creek, we can see upriver to Kyson Point, Sutton Hoo, Woodbridge and downriver towards the cranes at Felixstowe docks. Eight creeks. It's hard to envisage how the creeks and river work together. From where we stand, this inlet seems like a river itself. Our senses are engaged towards an ethereal place of sky, water and mud. The barriers of our everyday selves are softened, enabling us to access that liminal space between what we say and what we feel.

Our Autumn Walk remembers Dave. The wind is blowing from the west, warm as we sit to eat our snacks. Sometimes we talk altogether, sometimes in twos and sometimes we are alone.

TOWARDS WINTER

For the three of us, the river continues. We've completed eight journeys. For the ninth, we're at Ramsholt, an old fishing village on the northern shore of the river. This is a remote land of long, narrow access lanes margined by ploughed fields and wind-fashioned pines. When we started, we could have jumped over the Deben's trickle. Now, at high water, it's almost three hundred metres to the far side. As we move inland, three Canada geese rise from a grazing marsh but our path across is boggy and impassable. We have to skirt the field instead, past hedges of berries, rich and dripping with sloes. Harebells still bloom. Then, the startled thrill of seeing a Chinese water deer leaping over the meadow. All Saints Church, sentinel site for the Saxons perhaps, keeps watch as we sit beneath its flinted tower. The mirrors of time and river are holding still. I see how far I have come and, of course, I still have some way to go. But I know, even when the Deben reaches Felixstowe, when the ten walks are done, the quest will never really end there, will it?

A SUMMER OF SECRETS

ROWENA KILKELLY

The lid on the heavy black tin box opened with the help of a hammer, the lock already broken, swings from side to side. A label still readable, thick with dust and grime, hinted to a bygone era and the safe keeping of forgotten lives. I reach in and pull out bundles of letters, papers, statements, wills and photographs. Feeling the collapse of time, I fall down a burrow, on land once plagued by rabbits, where Kate, my great-grand-mother, is living. She is calling me, pulling me into her life, into her time and place. 'Can I tell you a secret?' she whispers as I step back beyond my past.

I find sunlight bursting through a canopy of oak, ash and chestnut trees; they line both sides of a long winding avenue, inviting family and callers up the stone steps to the front door of long-lost Coney Hall, Kate's ivy-clad home. A salty breeze from the Irish Sea, less than one mile away surrounds this house, ships crossing the sand bar at high tide, can be heard sounding their horns, as they sail up the river Boyne.

This is a tranquil, dream-like place, where horses snort and blow their noses impatiently. High above, leaves rustle and whisper, disturbed by black crows and sea gulls, playing 'catch me if you can!' Coney Hall, the house, parkland, gardens and farm no longer exist;

I become an omnipresent observer missing nothing. I have never been here in person. My great-grandmother died many years before I was born, yet now I feel at home here and imagine her saying 'welcome' as we come face to face.

***

It is mid-summer 1933, and the tall windows of this early Georgian residence reflect the sunlight so strongly that I am dazzled. I see Kate is standing there looking out, searching for answers to questions that have been troubling her of late. She is now seventy-seven years old and a widow for almost ten years. She is the mother of three daughters and one son. All her children have married well, and, just like Kate herself, her daughters have marriage settlements, so, if they wish, they can kick up their independent heels, whenever they feel the need.

Because Kate struggles to climb the broad staircase, her bed has been moved downstairs to the large, front drawing-room on the left side of the hall door, a vantage point for all the comings and goings of the house. Her three dogs sit close, alert to her mood, her voice and her gestures. Valuable images taken by Irish photographers, like Lafayette, engaged by the family, bring my ancestors to life. Kate is small in stature, warmly plump. Her soft white hair is piled neatly, using pins, on top of her head. In old age she is pretty, her bright, brown eyes twinkle. Fastidious regarding her appearance, her dress sweeps the floor as she moves, highlighting her waist and bosom. A small magnifying glass hangs from a gold chain around her neck. I read that, in the past, a seamstress has travelled from Liverpool to Coney Hall on Irelands east coast, to fill Kate's dressing room with the latest fashionable attire. Now she barely goes out. Her old bones are slowing her down, yet her mind is just as alert and inquisitive as always.

I become Great-grandmother's shadow. I am here, yet not here. I silently watch her, read her thoughts and listen, as life within the house ticks slowly by. We are joined by a shared history; she looks forward while I am looking back. She and I are spending this summer hour by hour, day by day, together, as she decides to change her will in favour of her daughters. As I dig deeper and peel back the layers, I feel her inner turmoil and her apprehension as she devises a secret plan to outwit her son. Will she carry it to fruition?

Kate's brow is furrowed with worry as she threads together her doubts about great-uncle John and the many occasions, in her eyes, when he has not behaved like a gentleman. He was once her favourite child. I lean in closer still and read her black thoughts, now a festering pot since the death of her husband, my great-grand-father James. She has read several newspaper accounts, local and national, where John has engaged in lawsuits with his wife Kathleen's family, one for slander, and the most recent for contesting Kathleen's father's will. With some trepidation, Kate has destroyed these newspapers and hopes they are not widely read. She also feels that John has done very well under her husband's will, even receiving more in stocks and shares then he ought, because the will was not strictly carried out at the time. Kate has kept all this to herself, now she is feeling the stress building daily and can think of nothing else. With her wisdom of age, she knows that life is uncertain and, as a woman, she considers it her duty to provide for her daughters, Frances, Alice and Catherine.

Behind the facade of Coney Hall, Kate's eldest daughter, Frances, enjoys living with her mother. Fifty-three years old, she is three years a widow and has no children. Her wedding in 1906 was a grand affair at Coney Hall. Her husband, Thomas Wafer Byrne, from a family of Liverpool jewellers, was a dental surgeon. Fashionable like her mother, her wedding dress was made of Irish lace with ostrich feathers adorning her head, and that same afternoon they left to honeymoon on the Continent, Frances wearing Irish tweed, and a smart green felt hat. For the following twenty-four years the couple lived on Prince's Street in Liverpool. During this 1933 summer of doubt, Frances spends time away from her mother, in Dublin and holidays in Connemara on Ireland's west coast. While at Coney Hall she helps to look after the house when her mother is feeling poorly; at times she practically manages the place. On occasions when Kate is feeling better, this leads to some friction between the two women. Sensitive and perceptive, Kate is afraid her daughter might leave and return to Liverpool. She has developed confidence in Frances and is beginning to lean on her more and more.

It is a notably warm summer with very little rain. Even with the open windows there is no cool air entering the house. Kate is suffering from a very weak heart and avoids making any physical effort. Within her bed-sitting room she attends to all business matters herself, paying her bills, advertising for 'a steady, respectable girl as laundress and plain cook' and for 'a general man for plain gardening, cottage provided.' She writes her letters, sending charitable donations to priests and nuns who care for the poor locally. She sets great store by dates and anniversaries, remembering birthdays and important events. Mentally, Kate is quite marvellous. Her outings sadly are almost at a standstill; in fact, this summer she only takes one short journey by motor car.

Her live-in nurse Marie McGann takes her out in a wheeled chair most days after lunch. They proceed down the new wooden ramp, with detailed wooden rhombus shapes; it extends down the right side of Coney Hall from the front door. Along with the dogs, they both enjoy freedom from the darkness and heat within the house, and take a different path each day. Straight ahead brings them along the avenue and beneath the trees where a horse might pick up its ears and lower its head over the iron railing, waiting for a cube of sugar. Or, turning right towards the farm, they may watch the chickens and ducks race to peck the same invisible speck. The farm labourers doff their caps and wave, a token of respect and affection for their mistress.

Turning left takes them to the high walled garden, where Kate likes to linger for a while; with eyes closed, she remembers walking arm in arm with her husband James. She imagines that lost riot of colour, with the intoxicating scent of red, white and yellow climbing roses, in fragrant competition with wild honeysuckle.

Perhaps she sees and hears her children, young again, playing hide and seek as, she herself delves further back in time. During these quiet moments together as they wend their way through the grounds, Kate never discusses her private thoughts with her young nurse, for fear that John might learn what she intends to do. Nurse McGann spends three summer months nursing Kate, yet they remain distant, as Kate believes the utmost secrecy is called for at all times. She will not lose her dignity.

Kate's second daughter, Alice, is my grandmother. I had the pleasure of knowing her for almost thirty years and indeed I loved everything about her. Softly spoken and smelling of lavender, I remember sitting at her feet as a child and learning to read each colourfully illustrated page of *Alice's Adventures in Wonderland* by Lewis Carroll. We would act out the story, speak in riddles, shrink in size, attend tea parties and steal the Queens's jam tarts. I remember her confiding, as one second child to another, that 'being a second child is difficult, but you will get through it, just as I did.'

In this 1933 summer of secrecy, my grandmother Alice is fifty-one years old. She is married to a veterinary surgeon, and they live just six miles away from Coney Hall, across the river Boyne in the town of Drogheda. Their wedding in September 1909 at Coney Hall was a colourful affair. The house was decorated with green foliage and garlands of flowers from the garden, banners hung across the road near the small church. The local population joined the wedding festivities on this warm sunny day, cheering as the couple passed in their Irish Jaunting Car.

Alice and Andrew have eight children ranging in age between nine and twenty-three. Coney Hall is the children's playground and several times a week they arrive by pony and trap. Six miles of trotting, with the wide river Boyne on their left side as the children look out for passing ships and take turns holding the reins. The pony sweeps a long tail from side to side, keeping flies away, then trots faster, almost gallops, up the tree lined avenue to where Kate is always at her window waiting, the dogs barking.

While the children ride ponies, climb haystacks and play, the adults have tea in the shade beneath the trees or just below the front steps. Kate's granddaughter Mary has a camera and photographs are taken. All the while, Kate tells no one about her worries over her plan to change her will.

Kate's third daughter and youngest child is forty-six-year-old Catherine. An apprentice solicitor before she married Arthur O'Connor, a Major in the British Royal Army Medical Corps in 1920. They have three young daughters and live far away from Coney Hall in India. Great-grandmother Kate insisted that her own daughters should experience everything that life could offer. They rode side-saddle and swam in the Irish sea. They attended a Dublin Catholic boarding school, playing both the piano and the Irish harp. All three speak French and they all spent time in Paris, attending classes at the Sorbonne. Trips across the Irish sea between Drogheda and Liverpool for shopping and race meetings were not uncommon and when low tide delayed the boat sailing up the river Boyne into Drogheda, a rowing boat from the beach near Coney Hall was sent out to row them home without delay.

Once her dearest child, Kate's son John is now fifty years old. A solicitor for twenty-five years, he succeeded to his father's practice in the firm of Smyth and Sons, Drogheda. He is a man of personal charm and is popular in every social circle. As a young man, John enjoyed hunting, point-to-point, riding, tennis, golf, fishing and shooting, indeed all the pursuits of a country gentleman. He enjoys farm management, presiding over a substantial farm; passed down from Kate's side of the family, just a few miles inland from Coney Hall. In his will, his father James bequeathed John the family's town house, number 41 Laurence Street, Drogheda, along with all the furniture, books and papers within.

This is a substantial three-story house with the legal practice attached. John lived with his mother until the age of forty-two when he married a medical doctor. They have three sons and resided in Drogheda for a number of years before moving to live in Dublin. John commutes the thirty miles between Dublin and Drogheda each day by train or motor car. His mother is now both critical and censorious of everything regarding John, yet she manages to remain, in his eyes, a loving and devoted mother; he suspects nothing and assumes that Coney Hall will one day be his. He has after all seen and is in possession of his mother's will, made shortly after his father's death. As an only son, primogeniture is still the custom and he is sure of his inheritance. Kate tells her doctor she is nervous, because she never knows when John will arrive at the house or when he will stay overnight, she is always on her guard.

In the midst of this hotchpotch, I begin to arrange my paternal ancestors neatly in and around the big house. I can see them all. The young photographer, Aunt Mary, has captured them forever; I see stolen moments of family life, calm, surprise and laughter. I see my aunts and uncles, my great-aunts and great-uncle, I see my great-grandmother. Kate is always centre stage, watching, sitting comfortably with a faint smile; I want to reach out and hug her tightly.

Her daughters sit together on a wooden wrap-around bench, which embraces an old chestnut tree snugly. Handsome women, wearing city suits and hats, grass growing beneath their stylish shoes. All three have light silk or cotton scarves thrown loosely on their shoulders and happily smile for the camera. They look alike and are at ease with one another. Tea is enjoyed at a garden table below the front steps, a tartan style tablecloth covers the table, a tray with teapot displayed, makes me want to join my ancestors for afternoon tea.

Great-uncle John is there too, standing; he wears riding breeches, a fitted riding jacket and knee-high polished riding-boots, a bowler hat fits perfectly on his head. In one hand he holds a lit cigarette, in the other a short riding crop, a wide smile on his face. I like him. Soon he rides away beyond the photograph on a splendid horse along with one of my young aunts on a small pony; they turn their heads laughing and wave to the camera.

Doctor Patrick McCullen had been attending Kate for many years and because of the nature of this present illness, he is now a very frequent visitor. Kate enjoys a great deal of trust with her doctor and holds him in the highest regard. Although she never asks his opinion, she constantly discusses her affairs with him. He records everything in detail, filling his notebooks. He always finds Great-grandmother keen and acute. In the course of these discussions Kate has on a number of occasions expressed her distrust of John and she makes it clear that she does not wish that he should know what she is doing in her affairs. She resents anything that might touch the good name of her late husband's legal practice.

From all these little chats, Doctor McCullen thinks Kate's attitude throughout is the attitude of a reasonable and sensible woman who is anxious, so far as she can, to keep her affairs out of her son's hands, without letting him know she is doing so. He thinks this is quite proper and understandable.

Desperate letters begin to fly both ways between Kate and her solicitor, Mr Branigan, who lives and has his office in Drogheda. The first from Kate dated 1st July, states she wishes to consult him on a very private matter, and he must on no account mention this to any member of her family. She tells him he must arrive by bus and not by hired car. Two or three days later Branigan steps off the bus and walks up the avenue.

Kate is waiting and watching from her window. Alone together in her room, she whispers and refers to the will and codicils already made. Dissatisfied with the provisions thereof, she tells him she now wishes to revoke them and make a new will. This new will must be made in simple terms, she has no wish in creating complicated trusts. She wishes to alter the provisions she has made regarding John. Her daughters are important now, especially Frances, who she thinks has been left unprovided for. Kate impresses on Branigan the need for the greatest secrecy, John must not find out. They are interrupted by a gentle knock on the door, afternoon tea is served and enjoyed at a small table near the open window. They discuss matters in general and before leaving to catch his bus, Branigan arranges to see her again in a few days to obtain more detailed instructions.

Kate can decide for herself what she wants to do regarding her will and her daughters. This is unusual, as women are rarely ascribed their own agency. She is entitled to certain property with a power of appointment under the wills of her father and husband and under her marriage settlement. I begin to understand that despite her age and illness, Great-grandmother enjoys a considerable force of character and nothing, except John, will stand in her way.

Kate confides in her doctor that she is a little afraid of John, and on one occasion she tells him 'John might lose his temper, and I am not able to stand that; my health is not good enough.' In order to dispel any doubts that John might have regarding Coney Hall, Kate draws up a codicil in John's favour and they sign it together, then when he leaves the house, she destroys it by throwing it into the fire.

———————

Kate and Branigan correspond almost daily. My deep black box reveals that Branigan keeps every letter, he records almost every conversation. Kate decides to use her old will of 1930 as a template, to alter and amend for the better. Using blue ink and a thin nib, she begins to change it line by line. Resolute and strong, she strikes a thread-like stroke through sentences, neatly writes notes in the margins and rewrites some paragraphs. I begin to notice Great-grandmother and Frances, whispering, heads close together. Frances looks over Kate's shoulder as she writes, corrects and writes again. Blotting paper always at the ready, there are no smudges, no blobs of ink. One word jumps out on each page, 'daughter, my daughter, my daughter Frances.'

Occasionally a verbal message is sent from Kate through her doctor to Branigan, but the gist of these Branigan can't remember. In mid-July he receives Kate's previous will, altered and amended, followed the next day by a letter requesting it to be returned for just one day, as she has forgotten some of the things and wishes to refresh her memory, adding that Frances wishes to see it too. I sense unease and tension everywhere within the house. Kate ends all her letters with two words, 'preserve secrecy or strictly private.' Frances is also, in my eyes becoming more and more involved in her mother's plan.

In early August, the hot weather tries Kate; she is a little short tempered with everyone including the dogs. When Branigan fails to arrive for an appointment, she is vexed, and writes immediately, telling him that John has not been to Coney Hall for some time, but he is due on Saturday night. She tells him while she is happy with the new draft, there are still a few issues to clear up. She implores him to come to the house the following Monday at 1.10pm to complete the document. She adds that she is not well and worries a lot about this important matter.

On the 18th of August, Kate writes to Branigan asking him to send the finished will at once, as she is not too strong, and she feels it should be executed. She writes, 'I trust I am not rushing you too much.' The following day the postman delivers a registered envelope to Kate; it is the new will and Branigan is clear in his accompanying letter how it should be validated. He tells her to sign it before two witnesses. He instructs that both witnesses should be present at the same time she is signing, and that they should both sign their names as witnesses in the presence of all three; she must also fill in the date.

With a thumping heart, and a feeling like ice-cold breath on the back of her neck, she quickly hides it beneath papers in her bureau. Frances is holidaying in the west of Ireland; she decides to wait and read it again on her return.

On the afternoon of the 21st of August, Kate is sitting at her desk in her room waiting for Doctor McCullen to arrive. She knows that Nurse is somewhere within the house, and that Frances is away for the day. Nervously, she reads her will several times, places it in the centre, on top of the bureau, next to her pen and ink bottle. She hears the sound of light feet running through the hall towards the front door. She then hears heavy footsteps climb the seven stone steps outside and McCullen is shown into Kate's room. Everything is ready at last.

They discuss the task ahead for several minutes, then Nurse McGann is summoned to the room and asked by Kate to be a witness to her will. Kate is the first to sign, then standing up, she moves aside, while McCullen and Nurse both sign in turn. Each is in full sight and in the full presence of the other. Nurse, without knowing or wanting to know the contents of the will, leaves the room, running down the back stairs to the garden for fresh air. Her time at Coney Hall is almost over.

McCullen listens to Kate's heart and checks her pulse, thinking to himself, 'She is absolutely competent to execute this will, and is as competent to do so as I would be myself.' He then takes his leave. When Frances returns, she checks the will and signatures, then together they hide it somewhere safe, where John will never find it.

Kate is at peace; her black cloud of worry has evaporated. Frances seeks out Nurse and tells her she is very annoyed at seeing her signature on the document, because nurses are not supposed to act as witnesses to a will and she might get into trouble for doing so. Two weeks later, Kate adds a codicil to her will and this time it is signed by McCullen and his chauffeur. Then the whole business is put to bed.

Three of the characters in Kate's drama live or work on Laurence Street, in the town of Drogheda. Kate herself was born and grew up at Farrell House on this handsome street. Branigan her solicitor lives at number forty-five, McCullen her doctor lives at number thirty-three and John's own legal practice is at number forty-one. I wonder, as they come and go during this 1933 summer of secrets, do they tip their hats, hide a discreet smile, salute each other with a 'good morning', 'good afternoon', 'good evening' or 'good night', then hurry away to implement Kate's wishes?

It is late September, and summer is over when I take my leave of Great-grandmother and Coney Hall. I feel she is exhausted and frail, the house growing colder and darker. The leaves on the trees are beginning to change colour and visits from family are reduced. Nurse has been replaced, and Frances is always away in her car or on holiday. The dogs sit still, watching and listening. There is silence all around Coney Hall.

I leave it all behind reluctantly and with a heavy heart. I place the bundles of papers back within the black tin box, close the lid and watch the broken lock swing from side to side. The voice of Kate herself and all those who spent time with her at Coney Hall that summer, are silenced again. I skip the generations and return to my own time and place. I am almost the same age as Great-grandmother Kate. I have four daughters of my own. There are no family secrets to find or discover, there are no traps set.

In the years between that summer of 1933 and Kate's death, her physical and mental health declined rapidly. When Branigan met her again four years later during the summer of 1937, she appeared much changed and to have failed greatly. Great-grandmother passed away in March 1939; she was eighty-three years old. She died fortified by the last Sacraments of the Catholic Church of which through her long life she was a worthy daughter.

Her will was a shock for John, a great shock he carried with him for the rest of his life. No child wants to be left out, and Kate was not shy in expressing that Frances was her favourite child. Naturally, he contested his mother's will, going all the way to the High Court. He claimed his sister Frances had used undue influence over his mother at a time when she was not of sound mind. The case was reported widely in all the national newspapers, something Kate would have deplored.

She bequeathed to her eldest daughter Frances, Coney Hall, the house, farm and land, the furniture, household goods and effects, all the stock, horses, crops, implements, cars, carts and motorcars, all chattels and things inside or outside. To her daughters Alice and Catherine, she bequeathed her properties and land within the town of Drogheda.

To John, she gave all the shares that were in their joint names at the time of and since her husband's death and in order to remove any possible doubts that might arise regarding these, Kate made a list. In her codicil Kate declared that if any person should dispute the validity of her will, that person will forfeit all benefits. John withdrew his opposition to the will at a sitting of the High Court when it became clear the outcome would not be in his favour.

Daughters are more likely to care for an ageing parent and in this case, it makes sense that they are more likely to be favoured in the will. After her mother's death Frances spent the winter months on the Riviera, and when in Ireland she lived in various hotels in Dublin. Ten years later, she sold Coney Hall and most of the contents. Some items were put into storage and there they remained for the next decade or so. Frances died twenty-three years after her mother, in a Dublin private nursing home, and was buried beside her in Drogheda.

The death of their mother led to long-held dormant differences between the siblings. John was the loser, and I suppose was left full of the most overwhelming series of emotions — anger, sorrow, love, remorse, hate, bitterness — all mixed together. That was Kate's bequest to her only son, these horrifying feelings that would never leave him.

It appears from letters that John may have upset his mother and sisters when he married late in life and left home. He had been the centre of attention and spoiled by everyone. His wife, a medical doctor, noticed very early on that Kate could throw a little faint when things did not go her way. She said all Great-grandmother needed was 'a drop of brandy'. This remark did not go down well with her new family. John's wife also let it be known that she thought Coney Hall was haunted, and she never wanted to stay there. These were all black marks for the future where Kate and her daughters were concerned. The earlier court cases were probably the final straw.

Was Kate arbitrary or capricious when making her will, slowly falling out with John? Whatever is written in a will cannot be unsaid and lays the foundation for future family disharmony. Once Kate's will was revealed, relations between the families soured until after John's death in 1954. Was great-uncle John judged unfairly by his mother? I believe he was. Despite her judgement, John was always the perfect gentleman to all those who knew him. He became one of the best-known members of his profession in Ireland, becoming vice-president of the Incorporated Law Society.

When John's son qualified as a solicitor and succeeded to his grandfather and father's practice in Drogheda, he was determined to restore relations with his aunts and meet the cousins he had never known. They all became great friends. As inheritance after inheritance spread out across the generations, Great-grandmother's legacy disappeared and who remembers? This story has been drowned out. It never puzzles or nags anyone; it is simply forgotten.

The practice of Smyth & Son, Solicitors, established in circa 1870, is still there with John's grandson part of the legal team. Red ivy-clad Coney Hall is gone and has become a sea of housing estates, with roads that criss-cross a landscape where a family home full of secrets once stood, where streams once flowed and giant trees once flourished.

If you stop, listen and look, ships still sound their horns as they navigate the river Boyne, dogs still bark, crows and sea gulls still fly. On my finger I wear a ring passed down to me from my godmother, the photographer aunt Mary, passed down to her from her godmother great-aunt Frances. I have been to a place now lost. I have wrapped my arms around family long gone. I have been home.

MOTHERLAND

CAREY SOMERVILLE

The car judders and sighs with me as I wind round the last lane, over the potholes and through the puddles, until I reach the bend in the road that leads home to my Essex plot, my small piece of fertile ground in the family promised land of over half a century ago.

A land too, in which I was once a sad and lonely child in a family of dark secrets and cold corners, where little girls might stumble into snares, and women lost their way.

Home: solid, safe, and warm — created and curated by generations of nameless, faceless and propertyless women whose stories vanish like dust in the surface shifts of history. A photograph hangs in my front hall, showing what the cottage was like when it was first built, the women who lived here standing in front of it. The women look warm and welcoming: here looks as if there is a space for me to rest and breathe.

I do not know their names.

Will they walk with me and help me carry the trauma on my back?

For I am the scapegoat. The one who has been given the load.

These are the women whose stories whisper through the cracks in time, speaking to my rural childhood, my instincts as a feminist historian, and my yearning for home. I stand in the garden and let stillness, silence and the scent of country flowers take the inner tension from the coiled, sullen child inside me, the child who unknowingly dwelt in a dysfunctional family and looked for mothering in the landscape.

She deserves this.

The earthy smell of my fertile front garden tugs me back to the feeling of being seven, on a farm less than five miles away.

We called my farming grandfather Dodo, for to us he was indeed an extinct old bird. But he was once a hawk-eyed bird of prey, hatched from Victorian aspiration. His family wore their wealth and status in urbanised propertied plenty: at one stage they owned half of Camden Town and kept a lion to symbolise their affluence.

The women, of course, owned nothing and have left no voice.

The dark and dangerous misogyny of my grandfather's childhood world reverberates in the darker parts of my own life — the parts that left me homeless, friendless, familyless: this is a world where the men wield the power and distort the world of the women and children.

My great-grandfather 'impregnated a maid' and disappeared to Australia, coming back to a sad marriage with my great-grandmother, which made home, however affluent, a place of madness and mayhem and resulted in five children damaged by his cruelty; one was my grandfather.

I once contemplated the roots of the family misery in a poem about my great-grandmother who stood beside my monstrous great-grandfather as his rage ripped through her offspring:

Violet Constance

Violet Constance-
Constant violence
The tone of your marriage
A monstrous contract by all accounts
Dogged by bitter dislike,
Enmity and emissions of cruelty
Which echo down the generations like the hard strike of Iron on Stone.
Iron, stone, metallic clangs,
Unyielding surfaces the interfaces of family life.

'I don't like little girls,' you said.

What Victorian daemon, unleashed, blindly forgot
The imperative of love?

The human touch
Of warm flesh, clasped hands, simple affection
Unrecorded, unmarked in that generation.

And we, your great-grandchildren,
Children, children's children
Feel daily this absence.

If I could walk back through all those years, hold their hands, and tell my forbears modern truths about intergenerational trauma, about the absolute necessities of childhood, I would.

My great-grandfather lined up four of his children against a wall and held a shotgun to them. He did not fire it, but all four suffered:

agoraphobia, alcoholism, bipolar disorder – dark and seeping wounds just beneath a modern skin.

And mopped up by the women.

The cold hand that handled weaponry against kin,
The hand you took in marriage,
Grasps the heart still.

Four lives shattered without a shot being fired.
They stood before the blast
Of an unfired gun
An explosion of unchecked, Cimmerian child-rage.

I recall them existing, Gollum-like
Under the volcano.

And always just beyond the last horizon
The family Nazgul
Like some perverted pet
Rides out to take us to the Mordor of the mind.

Where were you Violet Constance
Mother, missing when your children needed you most?

In coming home to my Essex country cottage, I am honouring the flickering remnants of Dodo's vision of rural peace and plenty in the Essex village of Thaxted, far from his city torments and enshrined in a 1938 film by the Boulting brothers entitled *The Ripe Earth*[1]. From the first, enticing shot in the film, wooden cartwheels frame a vision

---

1. https://eafa.ehost.uea.ac.uk/work/?id=2292

of bucolic glory: unfettered birdsong; abundant animal life; unmechanised harvesting of wheat sheaves in a landscape of meadows and eternally youthful, smiling grandparents.

My grandmother had joined my grandfather in this rural idyll, searching for her own sense of security. Her parents had been conscientious objectors in the First World War. Rejects from polite society. Outcasts who did not eat meat and went to prison for their pacifism. They did not enjoy the luxuries of peaceful plenty. And so here she was, settled with my grandfather's legacy in the relative comfort of farming life.

'It's all nonsense,' my father said of the film, which, in many ways, it was. The ritualistic mysteries of the Morris Dance which frame the film's vision, had been reconjured in the 1930s by Gustav Holst and Conrad Noel. Dark traces of the underbelly of want haunt the graveyards, the landscape, and the lives of my forbears. You can hear them if you listen to the single, melancholic violin which accompanies the Abbots Bromley, the all-powerful horn dance which gives the village its rural magic at midsummer.

But this is my History: as a small child, I wove my own meaning from the riches of our rural life and the lost love my grandparents found in the fields. The Anglo-Catholic and socialist folk tradition of the wider village still spreads its mystical spell through life's banalities.

The truths enshrined in this vision — the bonding and healing powers of food, fellowship, music, honest labour, and the love of the countryside — these are eternal truths, a rock to cling to when the hard fist of abuse comes for you.

It has taken me a lifetime to grow back into them and to find my own sense of comfort, created by my own hard labour.

My grandparents flew out from the city, instinctively re-homing, out into the alien haze of the rural dream. Utopian visions were conjured, redemptively, from the shadow of the First World War and were accompanied by an exultation of skylarks.

In my memories of harvest heydays, over half a century ago, there is an intensity — of dust, urgency, back-breaking labour. The men sweat dirt, the women arrive, freshly head-scarved and bearing baskets of home-baked and hungered-for food. The children run through the stubble and shriek and sing with excitement, their feral whoops compete with the mechanised roar of the combine harvester, the churn of other engines.

I can feel the precarious ecstasy of wallowing in the grain pumped into trailers, and climbing through stacks of straw bales, despite the punishing scratches and layers of dust and prickling husks inside all our clothing, even our underwear. The light is always golden, and our lives infused with the joy of surfing on the riches of life outside.

Later, when the Leviathan of change slayed my grandparents' dreams, my grandfather's life began to lose its intimacy with the nature which sustained him. The charms of rural meadows and tumbling hedgerows were crumbling beneath the drive to squeeze profit and productivity from them; my grandparents felt their idyllic life in rural arcadia slip through the cracks.

Now there was freshly smoothed concrete, new machinery for modern farming. After months of stumbling through the demands of 1960s mechanisation, my grandfather broke down on a perfect, rose-framed, English lawn, surrounded by neatly arranged sand-wiches and scones on Crown Derby China, lovingly prepared by my floundering grandmother.

The women and children hid the slow implosion of our homes' foundations through the banality of shallow chit-chat, resolute in the pretence of normality. Wide-eyed and hushed by my parents, I watched my grandfather's tortured mouth and expensive dentures, at odds with the lush sweetness of my grandmother's English tea.

His tears dripped.

The baby gurgled.

The apple trees bent towards them both, but their embrace went unheeded.

The last time I saw my parents' old farmhouse, it was shrouded in hushed, newly planted trees, hiding a place where a woman took her own life after we had left.

I was thrown out of that house one dark, wet day when I was small. I hid in a barn.

Back in the sixties it was a tumbling jumble of a place, part Elizabethan, part 1930s addition, three farm cottages forged together to make a substantial farmhouse. At its heart was a Tudor fireplace, framed with solid beams; the smoking heat was the centre of an otherwise chilly home. A pantry led through a back door to a kitchen garden, which intimidated my mother and which my father grassed over to create an image of middle-class respectability.

In my own small act of resistance, I adopted a harvest mouse which crept out of the 1960s Essex cold and into the orbit of fire, and I fed it scraps of supper in the dining room corner. One morning I found it dead in a mousetrap: squashed senseless by my parents.

There was still enough wild stuff out there to create a haven for a seven-year-old: nesting swifts and house martins in the pig barns; aconites and oxslips in shaded glades; a stream crossed by a fallen tree which wriggled with streaking sprinkles of stickleback and minnow. Like an entish wanderer from the ancient woodland less than half a mile away, was an aged horse chestnut, showering its pink-red panicles: a benign mother goddess.

Outside was a refuge. Inside my parents waged war: war with each other; war with their own 1930s childhoods; war with the roots of rural tradition. They barricaded themselves in with central heating, a stereo, en suite bathrooms. They forgot to guard against debt and frailty, to let the earth settle and settle the child in the garden.

I was bad, I was fat, I was in the way.

But outside I had my own world.

The family home, the family land, the family itself, have all gone in a cloud of debt, acrimony, agonised breakdowns. My seven-year-old self is still looking for them, for something that she can never have, and so has come home to the motherly embrace of my Essex workers' cottage.

The black and white photograph of my cottage in the 1880s presents a hopeful aspect where three women in black and white pose, proud and strong, in front of their solid, terraced cottages. The colour of their East Anglian straw-toned brickwork echoes the fields where their men are labouring, sweating their lives into the weeping ground. No smoke is coming from the chimneys, but you can imagine the blackened ranges, the open fires laid ready to welcome the family home.

You cannot see the back of the house where winds howl and whistle and sweep in from across the Fens, and there are overpowering stenches: animal manure and latrines, wash houses and cess pits. You cannot feel in your weary bones the hours of labour that keeping family and home would have required in the days before labour-saving devices. You cannot hear the conversations about paying the rent when the cash ran out.[2]

The front garden is filled with fruit trees, enough to feed the family through winter. The windows are new, and shine, opening wide to the south and the blessing caresses of the sun. Perhaps these women are proudest of their shiny slate roofs. A few yards away there is a row of thatched cottages which faces the threat, constant

---

2. Spike Mays gives a vivid picture of local Essex cottage home life in the history of his early twentieth century childhood. However, his account is questioned by local residents. Spike Mays, *Reuben's Corner*, (London: Eyre and Spottiswoode, 1969), Chapter 4.

for centuries, of the ravages of fire. Less than a decade before this photograph was taken, 'The Great Fire of Radwinter' in the neighbouring village destroyed twenty-four buildings and left ninety-five people homeless.[3]

The affluent Cornell family built these brick cottages in the 1880s: homes to raise children in, to feel safe and to prosper in the web of a rural community.[4]

Now these cottages house three teachers, a web designer, an office worker, a retired communications worker, and an army officer. The wider village houses two London taxi drivers and a variety of commuters who desert the place for a good twelve hours a day.

In 2024, the women are independent, professional, monied. And despite everything, I am one of them.

Thaxted lies across the fields. Sometimes the memories of its church bells bleed into the present moment. I am pulled back to its festival, to the spirit of the dance.

The cottage fronts have altered. The windows are all plastic, double-glazed, replacement versions. One cottage has been extended with a wooden frontage hiding the mellow Essex brickwork. One has been extended at the back with a bedroom which opens onto the ever-shifting glories of the East Anglian skies, their blues, greys and fiery reds, their scudding clouds, and the occasional glimpse of the resurrected wild: red kites.

This is my space.

Instead of confronting my own unresolved pain, I search for the

---

3. https://saffronwaldenmuseum.swmuseumsoc.org.uk/fire-brigade-history-timeline-19th-century/
4. I discovered this fact quite randomly when a Mrs Betty Bryning backed into my car in Tescos. When she came to my house, she said that the cottages used to belong to her husband's mother's family, the Cornells.

Victorian women in my photograph in official documents. The life of the mind has served me well, built me a career and a selfhood.

At brain level, I trawl through the census records to find these women. At gut level, visceral response tells me that, with an effort of imagination, I can feel their roughened hands, smell their sweat, hear their stories.

The healing comes from acknowledging the wound.

Are these women from the past knocking on the windows, like Catherine Earnshaw, crying for some form of recognition that this was their home, that they existed and cultivated this plot?

I feel for their hands in the rain.

My neighbour tells me that an unquiet spirit haunts her upstairs bedrooms, but I have never heard her. Was she a woman who died in childbirth? A victim of influenza or domestic abuse? A woman driven crazy by unfulfilled desires? Perhaps her scent will seep through the floorboards, climb through the lost years, and permeate the present.

The women who lived here have left me no evidence, but there are clues about the realities of nineteenth century working class women's home life in local histories.[5]

I can feel their children's small hands like paper, a wind gust away from effacement.

Shock. Grief. Shifting ground beneath us. My children still mourn the four bedroomed detached house we lost twenty-seven years ago. All the solidity of its red brick frontage could not stop the fires of

---

5. Robert Gibson, *The Annals of Ashdon*, (Chelmsford: Essex Record Office Publication, Early 2000s?), P130 and Isabel Wiseman, *Wimbish Through the Centuries*, (Chelmsford: The Tindall Press, 1954), Chapter 9.

my ex-husband's alcoholism. I threw him out, he lost his job. We lost our home and had to pack up and leave, to fit into an alien and urbanised plot not of our choosing. My memories are of weeping over countless boxes, stacked for weeks, as the law lumbered on somewhere out of hearing.

There was worse beyond this. My family and my community supported my ex-husband. I was a harridan, a banshee. They tried to have me locked away. And then my brother beat me up.

Why?

Because, in the family script, my place is in the wrong. And out in the cold.

I picture my children's climbing frame, a rusting wreck in the lost garden, its once sturdy structure disintegrating with age and neglect.

How did I, an educated and independent woman find myself in this place, as marginalised as the women of the past?

I realised that I had no sense of self and no idea where to look for it.

Rack and ruin... the echoing rumble of intergenerational trauma is never quite out of earshot, even in my Victorian, hobbit-hole home.

It took me half a lifetime to realise that my home life was shaken by things that happened years, even centuries ago... the Irish stink which clung to my mother however hard she ran from it.

There was a silence in the space where family reunions, family love, should have been. In all my childhood, I visited the Irish family twice. They never visited us. The 'Irish shame' lurked just beyond our line of vision. I used to draw endless pictures of impossibly large families, naming all my missing cousins: John, Jane, Barry, Samuel, Elizabeth, Gladys, Kaye, and the others who were lost somewhere in my mother's closed address book. Where had she hidden them and why? What unnamed trauma was she attempting to heal with her daily Babette's feasts?

She cowered in a cupboard and shrank from the everyday irritants of life on a farm: rats, mice, dirt. Fear was central to her life. Fear of disease, fear of authority, fear of the madhouse.

The 'workhouse' had finally disappeared in her childhood, but the horror of it, like a maddening stench, drove compulsion and control in many of her generation.

My mother lives on in my home through her needlework. I sometimes wonder if she is the ghost, lost in the wrong attic.

Her curtains speak:

'Affluence, ease, grace: escape.'

Her desires and dreams still evident in the comfort in which I have clothed myself.

Tell me of the lives of women,
Woven with war-like wiles,
Subliminal sorrows empower their vision
Wreathed with winsome smiles.

Our woeful way from the sin of beginning
According to the lies
Of male-fuelled madness, truly chilling
In unrecorded trials.

I wonder often how to listen
To neglected, jewelled lives
Which whisper in embroidered linen
And are closed in dusty files.

My mother shimmies out of my sumptuous curtains, speaking through tumbling, salmon-coloured peonies on lined silk in tones she never used when she was alive. Soft lines, sibilant folds in the summer breeze — these and a few fading photographs the fragments left of a life somehow reclaimed by the Irish stubbornly rooted poverty.

'Mum, what next?'

I still find myself calling for her when stressed. But she is lying under her snowy covering. If I cried to the moon all night, she would not hear, she would not come.

'You're mad in the head,' she said.

I thought I must be, because my mother said so.

But I was not. It was she who spent twelve of her last eighteen months in a hospital for the mentally ill, and spiralled off on her final journey behind unforgiving, plastic, hospital curtains, shivering and ill-equipped to go.

'Will you say a little prayer for me?' she asked towards the end.

She was starving her body and shrivelled in her soul, Benjamin Button in an oversized hospital bed.

The Office for Statistics Regulation reports academic studies and research articles which indicate that Northern Ireland has the highest incidence of mental illness in the UK. Psychiatric morbidity in Northern Ireland is twenty-five percent higher than in the rest of the UK.[6]

Trauma theory suggests that this legacy has roots in the 'pishogue': the Irish famine. Professor Oonagh Walsh argues that the severe nutritional deprivation in the Irish in the famine years between 1845 and 1850 triggered 'epigenetic change' and that trauma has been passed through the generations as a result.[7]

This feels true to me, a lived experience behind the curtains in my childhood home.

My mother was permanently frightened of something just out of hearing. She was stitching her way to safety. If she could store up enough luxury at home, we would all be safe.

The threads of this fear are woven into our bodies, which carry with them the memories of Irish suffering: the nagging itch of eczema, the muscular moan of misused knees, the plangent reiteration of ancient residual lung problems.

Mental illness has only recently become socially acceptable. In the dialogues of my childhood and the histories of too many women, it was a shameful, hidden horror.

But the truth of the matter was this: my mum had a recognisable disorder and came from a family haunted by mental ill health. Her farming father hovered in a shroud of depression; I can picture him seeking the comfort of the kitchen range. Her younger sister died in a mental hospital, looking for something lost in some past life.

My memory of Auntie Olive is of her running across a cobbled yard, banging a stable door.

For my mum, illness was a means of creating meaning: Mum kept me at home 'sick' for large chunks of time, enfolded in her domestic control, her curtains of 'care'. Days and days of dozing on sofas while she was busy festooning her country houses, bought

---

6. https://osr.statisticsauthority.gov.uk/publication/review-of-mental-health-statistics-in-northern-ireland/pages/2/
7. https://www.irishcentral.com/news/irish-famine-mental-illness-connection

with my father's fevered quest for wealth in the heady 1960s and 70s.

Last summer, I went back up the long, winding track, back to my mother's first home, acknowledging some of my most intense longings for motherland. Like many Irish houses abandoned when a family moves on, it was derelict... a ruin, with a tree growing out of the remains of the stone walls.

In my photograph, the scowl of the Irish skies is a cowl over the lone tree bent in the wind. All that's left among the rubble is the gooseberry bush, still bearing the 'goosegogs' which Mum talked about in better times, with an echo of the childish glee she had somehow lost.

And there, smack, like a slap from the Atlantic winds, fragments of stories, retold by my rediscovered cousins, slot into the holes in my home life with a sadly satisfying fit.

Secret number 1: The family's babies are all still under the gooseberry bush, for Granny did not mother them. She was out on the fields, labouring. Auntie Kathleen fed baby Olive when she could, with a bottle of formula. Like Jeannete Winterson, I came to have empathy for the baby inside my mother: 'Only later, much later, too late, did I understand how small she was to herself. The baby nobody picked up. The uncarried child still inside her.'[8]

I came across these words with a shock of recognition: how much easier to acknowledge the pain of it through someone else. I must pick up my own uncarried self.

Secret number 2: The witchery that I used to suspect lay in my mother's heart had a family root. Uncle Cecil lay suffering with Bright's Disease and Granny came off the fields to treat him with Witch's Broom.

---

8. Jeannette Winterson, *Why be Happy When You Could Be Normal?*, (London: Vintage 2012).

Family love was inextricably linked with sickness, and the power of life and death lay with the witch who watched over the suffering.

Secret Number 3: The bindweed of family expectation choked the lives of the women. Auntie Kathleen scored the fourth highest result in the 11+ in the whole of Ulster but was not allowed to go to grammar school or, later, train to teach. Mum was made to leave school at fourteen, escaping at seventeen to the lure of nursing in Belfast and her own form of self-empowerment. Grace ran to America. Olive married an alcoholic.

Ragwort, thistle, dock and wild oat[9] creep round the foundations of the old Irish family home and whisper the sadnesses that my body must reconcile.

***

My uncle drives me back from the wild to the hearth in my aunt's kitchen. Here I drink in tea and family with thirsty gulps, revelling in acceptance and familiarity. The smell of the fields, rich with heavy rainfall, an Irish mulch of cow dung with undertones of peat, takes me back to my six-year-old self.

The ash trees flourish on the riverbank, and weeds wave in unsullied water.

My cousins' eyes, bones and teeth are so uncannily close to my mother's that I can feel her.

Hot tears come and that is all.

***

I can picture them at work and celebrate their chutzpah.

Back in England, I contemplate the strong countrywomen who

---

9. https://www.netregs.org.uk/environmental-topics/land/japanese-knotweed-giant-hogweed-and-other-invasive-weeds/invasive-plants-your-legal-responsibilities-in-northern-ireland/

have made my current home safe. I can feel my way into that strength.

Research has indicated that it was the character and strength of hardy working-class women which kept Victorian rural homes from disintegration and degradation.[10]

I would like to know more of their dreams and fantasies, more of the songs they sang to their children. I would like to trace their hot tears at the end of the day.

Soot. Smears of black on white caps and aprons, trampled into rugs, clinging to curtains, an acrid aftertaste in every meal. Fires were salvation and damnation rolled into one.

Carried by the East Anglian winds and fogs, coal dust crept into the best kept houses and women spent much of their lives fighting the fall-out of the flames which kept their families alive. At the back of my cottage there would have been a large copper or zinc tub, bubbling and boiling and seething with its brew of underwear and bedding. Blackened curtains would be soaked in salt water once a fortnight before being added to the broth.

The cold detachment of books cannot flesh out past lives, but it warms my heart that research is now unpicking the ingenuity and inherent value of the lives of ordinary women.[11] These lives can speak louder now, even through their vulnerability and powerlessness.

I am thankful to them, for the solidity of their lives is embedded in the solidity of my walls. I am resilient. I am resourceful. I am bonded to them.

In this space, I can celebrate my own chutzpah.

---

10. Nicola Verdon, *Rural Women Workers in 19th Century England*, (Woodbridge: Boydell, 2002).
11. https://www.cam.ac.uk/research/news/what-19th-century-women-really-did

Instinct leads me to find a girl who lived and worked here.

There is a 1940s photograph in Gordon Ridgewell's[12] book about my village, of what looks like the back of my cottage and two members of the Kidd family. In 1877, Thomas Kidd married Harriet Cornell (a member of the family who owned the cottages, one of whom was living at the end of my terrace in 1949) and they raised five children, a family of woodsmen, carving a living in tune with natural growth.

Fanny Kidd has left a sampler dated 1901.

She, at least, found a space to be creative.

<hr>

My cottage is a refuge and a portal: a place to write and to rest and to return to the haven that I found in nature as a child, to my grandparents' vision and to the Irish love of land. I lie in bed and listen to the plish of rain which runs in rivers down nearby Pounces Hill. But we are safe, warm: snugly tucked in a place built to last and paid for by labour at the chalk face.

Rats still use the old network of the cess pits as runs to race for chicken feed, but the thick walls keep them out. I am content to watch them defiantly gaze at me from the kitchen garden. A diminishing host of wild birds chatter and breed, fight, and feed — robins, blue tits, magpies. Sometimes at night the sound of ghosting owls threading the night sky makes my heart sing with hope that our native wildlife will survive.

Out in my generous labourer's plot, I am planting trees. The soil is rich, full of worms and organic waste. This is thanks to the generations of women who came before me: their chickens, pigs, and kitchen waste; I am reaping what they sowed and bless them in their

<hr>

12. All this information is to be found in the fantastic resource that is the local history produced by Gordon Ridgewell and his late wife, Megan — Gordon and Megan Ridgewell, *Sewards End: A History*, (Saffron Walden: G&M Ridgewell, 2010).

anonymity. Through the long years of rural recession, the impingements of war and change, the blessings of land would have kept their families fed. This is my grandparents' 'ripe earth' and a home for my smallest self.

Inside my rose-framed, book-filled haven, my grandmother's Crown Derby China flashily asserts its gorgeous gold and black splendour from the homely rustic dresser. My flame effect gas fire hoodwinks the senses in its solid, fake Victorian frame; I am thankful that it is clean and safe. The comforting swoosh of the dishwasher and washing machine a familiar background hum; life will continue tomorrow with cutlery and tableware, with clean clothes and containers for packed lunch.

A mothered household.

Et in Arcadia Ego.

With a woosh of internalised noise, this conjuror's trick evaporates.

In 2024, safety, security, the permanence of home are all just an illusion: the world outside reflects the inner noise of disquiet which has whispered to me since I was a small child in my frightened bed.

The echoes of family trauma still erupt like boils beneath the skin when the surface is scratched.

The incessant rumble of the M11, just over six miles away, thunders its warnings, even through my newly planted fruit trees. Overhead, the planes from Stansted circle like the lost starlings, their murmuration a dark shadow over the Garden of Eden.

And so many women are still lost.

Still, I am feeding my gooseberry bush with compost and dancing my way through the roses. The children and I are planting onions, garlic, potatoes amongst the established rhubarb, strawberries, and blackcurrants, and benignly watching the brambles and ground elder thread their memories of feeding mouths in hungrier times through the otherwise ordered flower beds.

We are leaving the front lawn to grow wild.

Dark Tea of the Soul

Klaudia Zotzmann-Koch

Crash!

I sat upright. The teapot! I *knew* it. My partner stood up, switched on the lights. A black shadow flew up the staircase and down the hallway. I heard sighing, then running water and wet cloth on wood. Tears gathering in my eyes, I went downstairs and, of course, there it was, in a thousand pieces: my grandmother's teapot, lukewarm tea I intended to drink the next morning darkening the towel my partner was mopping the floor with. Sobbing, I watched him collect the pieces into a pink plastic box. So many pieces. Pink check pattern on one side, sixty years of tea patina with a fine crackling web on the other. They rattled against each other in the box I held to my chest, just as I held the teapot when I left my grandma's house on the day of her funeral, my home for so many years, now inhabited by strangers.

Each day I made tea in Grandma's teapot and — paired with a cup on a wooden breakfast board — transported it up to my desk or to the small table by the sofa. And now the black kitten had made his first kill. The tea-bag-string must have snagged his curiosity. I can imagine him playing with it, pulling the white paper flag with his teeth, and his own shock when the teapot fell and shattered. He's a constantly anxious little fellow and usually means no harm. Nevertheless, I was devastated.

Crying was not going to make the tea pot whole. With the last of my tears it became clear what could. *Kintsugi*. I was going to learn the Japanese art of mending things with gold. I have always loved those objects with their shimmering defects. Defects that add to and transform beauty. And, if done right, restore functionality.

First thing in the morning, I grabbed my phone and — still in bed — searched for a kintsugi course in town. I found one. The teacher insisted on a phone consultation even though the course itself was to start over six months later, in May 2022. She asked if I had experience repairing things? Any talent for crafts? Skilful hands? She said, it was because the material, *urushi* lacquer, differed greatly from instant or two-component adhesive or whatever else one might find in craft shops. I suspect she was preparing me for disappointment, were things to fail.

The Puzzle

It was in a small and slightly crammed workshop that I took the lid off the plastic box, daring to peek inside for the first time since the night the teapot shattered. Sixteen pieces. Fewer than those in my memories. But many more than the three parts the teacher recommended for a first kintsugi piece. Nevertheless, she seemed optimistic — more than she actually was, as I learned months later — and we got started.

Maybe that's the one thing I have in common with my Grams. She led an unrooted life. Growing up and into her early twenties in a small town in Silesia as the youngest of seven children, she worked in a yeast factory and later at the Deutsche Reichsbahn. I remember her telling me so many stories of home — her home. Back before the war that changed everything.

When the Russian army started launching bombs into the city, Grams and her family were given two hours to vacate. Thanks to my grandma's job, they were allowed to take a box, a wooden crate packed with some clothes, a pot of lard, two dead chickens in a sack — but not their passbooks. They thought they would return in a couple of days. With their meagre belongings, Grams and her mother fled on a train; Grams standing outside on a footboard, wearing three dresses, one on top of the other, hair singed by the sparks of the steam engine in front. In Kirchmöser, they stayed with her oldest sister for a while, her father arriving too, with nothing but his leather document bag and a tin lunchbox which belongs to me now. I keep it, just two metres away from the teapot, in a drawer. I've always had a thing for travel mugs and dishes. Perhaps because of Grandma's stories of being on the run.

Grams settled in the German Vorharz region, where my grandfather and his family lived. She had been there with some friends before the war — twelve girls who travelled together to a little village because they liked its name. Her parents, not so much. Especially since their daughter desired to leave town and work somewhere else. Her father locked her hand cart in the basement so she wouldn't be able to get her luggage to the train station, but one of the girls loaded it onto hers and off they went — without her parents' consent. I admire the courage that must have taken, especially in 1938. I don't know if they knew of the local canning factory before, or if they looked for work on arriving in the village. However, it was in the factory that she met my grandfather. It must have been in May, for they canned asparagus. She recounted with pride, 'I was the fastest asparagus peeler!' The girls stayed on in the village for months. The canning of asparagus turned to peas, carrots, beans, mushrooms and cucumbers; until all workers were laid off at the end of the season. Grams worked at the sugar factory for a short while, then returned home — probably in December of the same year — where she started to work at the Deutsche Bahn. Grandpa rejoined the army in August 1939. During the war, he was tasked with bringing a prisoner to Glatz in Silesia, approximately 130 kilometres from Konstadt (close to Breslau), where Grams and her family lived. He decided to visit her and they were engaged in early February 1941. She had to leave town in January 1945 when Russian troops started bombarding. So when the war was finally over a few months later, because of their engagement, she had somewhere to go.

Replace Missing Pieces

Bottom and spout, an easy win. The upper half patched together too, with adhesive strips. Then, this hole in the teapot's belly and a whole handful of tiny pieces. The pink check pattern no help at all, impossible to align. A week and several hours of pondering later, it all matched, but for two missing pieces.

Where would *I* go? What would I do if my world descended into chaos? My parents still live in that small Vorharz village, around the corner from Grams' house. Grams' house... my home... my home no more. Would I return to the bigger house my parents built in the seventies? Perhaps. But, what of the strangers in Grams' house — my uncle's tenants? Would I be able to bear them there?

My own feelings of rootlessness began early on. A first childhood friend and her family moved to the next village, five kilometres away. I remember asking my mom where on that big, lit-from-the-inside globe she had gone. Clearly, five kilometres was an insurmountable distance for three-year-olds, for I never saw her again. When I was five-years-old, my grandfather died and Grams was never quite the same. But she stayed in her house, her garden. With me.

Grief is love with nowhere to go. She put hers into the garden. And me.

When I started school, she would take me to the bus stop every day. In winter, she would take me on my sleigh. After one year, an area reorganisation forced a change of schools. I lost most of the friends I had made. Three years later, grammar school was done, and another change loomed. Two years of intermediate followed, and yet another change.

Filling the Cracks

The teacher lent a hand, actually two. Weeks of glueing with a mixture of raw urushi lacquer and spelt flour, filling with a mixture of raw urushi lacquer and alumina, sanding, filling, more sanding...

What stayed? Most memorably, the fall of the Berlin wall during second year of intermediate school. Mom woke me up early one morning, saying: 'The wall is gone!' I wondered why I hadn't heard the lorry that must have driven into our garden wall, tearing it down, but soon realised she meant a totally different one. It was the wall I knew from visiting my great-uncle, Grams' only surviving brother, in East Berlin. When the war ended, he disembarked in Rostock from the submarine, the *Gneisenau*, on which he was the ship's carpenter. The wall that made us wait for hours at the border. The wall that looked like the barb-wired *Todesstreifen* (death strip); where at the age of four, a family friends' daughter and I had learned the difference between left and right, watched over by guards, their rifles trained on us. Our parents had stuck big, red dots on one of our hands, and told us to do exactly as they said, 'The side with the dot is right, the one without is left. When we say, "go right" or "go left", you do as we say. That's important. It's really dangerous here.'

I was more scared than I'd ever been. On the upside, I've never mixed left with right.

From the age of twelve, I lived with the feeling of being excluded. Even at the *Gymnasium*[1], where I had three girls in my class who I could count on as friends. But we all lived in different places — one in a village seven kilometres away, another in a town twenty kilometres away and the last in the city where we went to school, 25 kilometres from where we lived. Meeting outside school hours was a rare treat. But during all those mostly lonely times, I always had my Grams and our garden.

After university, I went to Vienna. I still hear my grandma saying: '*Das wirst du noch gereuen.*' (You will regret this.) I never did. I learned so much in Vienna. Met my ex-husband and subsequently my now partner. I know for sure I would not be the person I am, had I not had the opportunity to grow outside our small Vorharz village. But it still calls to me...

Layers

After weeks of filling and sanding the coloured urushi lacquer, a layer of black that cured for several days, then another of red...

That small patch of land somewhere in northern Germany where nearly my entire childhood is planted: a warm summer day, blue sky with fluffy white clouds, the sweet smell of fruit trees — plum, damson, mirabelle, cherry, apple, pear. Bees humming, butterflies dancing, birds singing all around. My grandpa is with me in the garden, Grandma looking out of the window, smiling. I'm maybe two years old. Chimes in the air — the ice-cream van is here! Grandpa hands me a coin. I run to the gate, stretch all the way up

---

1. German 'Gymnasium': secondary school that prepares for higher education.

and swap the coin for a scoop of ice-cream: woodruff. Light green and sweet and wonderful.

After summer comes autumn and brings with it hazelnuts and vetches at the compost bin. We lay potatoes on the fire Grandma has made from dried potato plants. The wind gets colder. Smell of frost on fallen leaves fills the misty air. Snow falls, and we play outside with the dog, fur crusted with snow, white and steaming instead of its usual rough and brown. Ice and snow turn into water, soaking the ground; snowdrops colour a whole patch white again, followed by daffodils, chives, peppermint, lilacs and all the fruit trees are in full bloom.

None of it exists anymore. Replaced by a deep yearning that gnaws at my soul. After Grandpa's death, they took down the trees, one after another. The last ones, including the big apple tree, felled years after I had moved to Vienna. Pain as fresh as on the day I saw it prone. Roots severed like my own. Some part of me died that day. I screamed at my mother — why had they killed my garden? I never forgave them. Nor returned to that now dead patch of land.

I once read that people plant gardens where there is hope; image of a better future — or at least, some kind of future. My grandma built hers on the memories of a home in a small town, a town that now bears a Polish name. She mourned her brothers and her past, as I mourn her and my past from a city nearly a thousand kilometres away.

Perhaps it is not my task to rebuild our lost garden. Going back feels strange. Going forward, a clean cut, a new beginning some-where not here. Although it's hard to accept, it feels like the wiser approach. But deep inside I still hope once again to live in Grams' house. For now though, all I have and treasure, is a fruity, earthy fragrance that changes with the weather and the seasons.

I didn't entirely inherit Grandma's 'green thumb'. I have a box of seeds: tomatoes, carrots, salad, chives, poppy and more, for my own garden, which currently is only a balcony with some flowerpots and boxes. For a long time, I kept a few apple seeds from the last apple off Grandma's tree. I don't know if they would ever have germinated. The chance of finding out gone with the little brown paper bag I stored them in, all claimed by the move from my now ex-husband's house.

Last year I was eating an apple, shop-bought, when I saw that one of its seeds had a little white tail. I put it in a flowerpot, and it grew, sprouted a few leaves. A little miracle. I managed to keep it alive over the much-too-hot summer. Then the flood came, followed by several weeks of drought. All the while my partner and I were not in town. My little apple plant didn't look too good when we returned. I will have to plant again.

Silver Dusting

On top of the two layers came a third: one more black, not fully cured, but dusted with real silver powder that sinks into it a bit. Another week of curing went by.

It took all my strength to attend Grams' funeral. I stood outside the chapel, unable to go inside. Going inside would make it real.

It was a cold and windy day in February, tiny snowflakes whizzing through the air. I sat numbly on the bench. Walked numbly to her grave. The one next to my grandfather's. The one Grams and I had visited together so often.

Her coffin was lowered into the dark soil and when they pulled out the ropes that held it suspended, the wind stopped. The snow stopped. Everything stopped for a second. Then, the clouds parted and the sun came out. As if Grams wanted to send a signal that everything was okay. She was with my grandfather again. She was home.

After lunch with the family, I went to her house, my uncle's house now, and took the teapot. It was the last time I went there. It was the last time I felt at home anywhere.

Polishing

The final step is polishing the metal surface. The teacher gave me a fish's tooth and after an hour, gently rubbing every crack, my teapot shines, kintsugi magic.

For years, I asked myself what I was doing wrong. Everyone I knew had grown up, found their people, settled into 'a home'. They were where they needed to be. I was still adrift, still searching... or perhaps I wasn't searching at all. Holding on too tight instead, to something that was no more.

Like Grams? She never forgot her home in Silesia. Talked so much about it, that it seemed half her soul was still there... in the living community where her father had played the trumpet up on the church tower for Christmas, in the neat town square, the usual trade shops all around, like the butcher's above which she and her family lived. People said, a *'Deutschenhasser'*, a German-hater, lived there after the war. He probably still lived there when Grams went back once in the 1990s — reluctantly — with my uncle. I remember her crying afterwards.

My cousin went in 2023 and sent pictures. Still exactly as Grams had described, frozen in time, ninety years on. The faded colours still say 'Schubert' over the shop window on the ground floor. They'd lived over that shop. Her mother had worked as household help for the owner. The outhouse is gone. There are more cars and a mobile phone shop on the corner. And plenty of dirty streets with some of the old houses boarded up — neglected and raw like my garden without its trees.

How I would have liked to keep it all as it was. Instead, there are overgrown brown shrubs, a car park, plastic toys and a trampoline. No trees. No bird-feeder. No care.

Maybe people are right when they say home is where your loved ones are. Maybe saying goodbye is a skill you have to learn. Leaving was hard, but maybe staying would have been harder.

The restored teapot has adorned the kitchen table ever since, far away from the edges. But I don't dare use it. Yet. The silver cracks have darkened, as silver does, when not in use. It sits here on the table, where I work and eat, a constant reminder of a home I no longer have.

Perhaps I need not hold back anymore. Like my portable apple tree, perhaps home is right here, where I'll find the courage to make tea in a once-shattered pot, pour it into a travel mug... and breathe.

ACKNOWLEDGMENTS

This anthology began when a collection of strangers, each with stories to tell, came together on a course in creative non-fiction at Cambridge University's Institute of Continuing Education (ICE), each bringing a unique voice, perspective, and passion for storytelling.

What we least expected, but all now treasure, was the creative community we found in each other. Over months of writing, reading, rewriting and sometimes doubting, we became a group, bound not only by the course, but by genuine connection, shared vision and mutual respect.

In each other's texts, we discovered new ways of seeing; in each other's feedback, we found clarity and confidence. This book exists because of the bond the ICE Pack has formed.

What lies herein has been shaped in no small part by the insight and generosity of those who guided us through months of learning, and whose thoughtful suggestions helped shape each piece with care:

Patrica Debney,
Louise Foxcroft,
Jessica J. Lee,
Derek Niemann,
Jane Rogoyska.

Thank you for your encouragement, your honest feedback, and your ability to challenge us with both rigour and kindness.

Sincere thanks also to Cressida Downing and Margaret Kirk for your keen attention, editorial insights and subtle nudges.

Finally, our deepest gratitude to Cambridge University. From creating the space for our further development to championing our final product, your support throughout the course and in the launch of this anthology has been invaluable.

About the Authors

Jo Cross lives and writes in Worcestershire, surrounded by fields, orchards and wooded slopes. It is a very long way from the sea. Having grown up sailing, she'd always imagined a life entwined with the sea, braided like a rope with all the other various strands of her life. But it was not to be. She writes about the gap between an imagined life and the lived one, that lingering sense of a road not taken.

After a varied career that encompassed social work, heritage management and setting up and managing her own coffeeshop/bookshop, Jo is now enjoying the time for more creative pursuits such as songwriting and wordsmithing. The beautiful Worcestershire countryside provides ample inspiration for her writing life.

Jan Fuscoe is a London-based feature and travel writer who, thanks to family connections, has spent a lot of time in Italy. She generally raves about Naples, Genoa, and Sardinia. Since the death of both parents, *Hiraeth* was an opportunity to write about her father (born of migrant Italian parents), adult loss, and memory, and one's own mortality. This is her first foray into creative non-fiction. Her next project is to write about her mother, who was born in Ireland. 'Because if we don't write about them, who will?' www.janfuscoe.com

Chris Hayward has been writing since she was a child, across a range of genres, formal and informal. In more recent work, she aims to link her inner and outer worlds, using the beauty of the written word as a liminal conduit.

Chris has degrees in English, Social Work and Management, plus qualifications as a teacher and headteacher. She has worked across the public services in Probation, Social Care, Health and Education. The sense of other is ever present in her work.

The inspiration for this piece of writing in '*Hiraeth*' has come from collaborating with a group of talented writers grown from the University of Cambridge. '*River*' is a juxtaposition of the practical and the personal: the parallel worlds of a walk along a river and a partner managing a serious health condition, together with the thin space in between.

Mana Jay is a multi-genre writer based in an idyllic London village that is often the star of her tales. Writing was her road not taken. When the Covid virus hit reset on the world, she had her own reboot going on to study creative writing at Cambridge. From non-fiction to fiction, from collective storytelling to solo ventures, Mana embraces opportunities to create and craft any where, every where. In *Hiraeth*, she explores the notion of belonging through people and place.

Having written on several upcoming anthologies, she is currently penning her deeply personal, poignant and at times painful memoir; a piece of writing she hopes will bring solace to some and understanding to others.

www.manajay.ink

Rowena Kilkelly is an Irish writer who lives on the edge of the Atlantic Ocean on Irelands west coast. A Masters in Women's Studies followed by two creative writing non-fiction courses with Cambridge University sparked a love of writing. Her inspiration comes from the wind that blows in from the sea, from Ireland's past and from her own ancestors, from the ground under her feet. She is currently working on a collection of short stories.

Pauline Hallam Mason came late to academia fulfilling a long-held ambition, after raising three children and working in business and academic administration. She obtained a BA in Philosophy at the University of Nottingham and an MA in Gender and Culture at the Central European University in Budapest. Then she spent two years from 1999 teaching English Literature at Yerevan Linguistic University, Armenia. During her time, in this new republic transitioning to democracy, she struggled to understand the people's constant mourning of exile and genocide over centuries. Now living in the United States and retired from her teaching at the University of Maine she has come fully to understand. A voluntary exile, she yearns to return to live in the land of her birth, especially since studying creative writing courses at the Institute of Continuing Education where she met this wonderful group of writers.

Barbara McMillan was born in Atlanta, Georgia and has spent most of her life in rural south Alabama, a region most famous for its flaws. She loves the Southern story-telling tradition of laying reality bare. Barbara, a retired psychology and sociology instructor, has a unique perspective on society and social dynamics. Having studied creative non-fiction writing at Cambridge, she writes about her understanding of the world around her, things we can relate to, but also things that take us by surprise. Still a practicing licensed professional counsellor and free-lance continuing education course writer, she dedicates a large chunk of her time putting her observations into words. In *Hometown,* she strives to make sense of life in her small community, if such a thing is possible.

www.barbarawritesnonfiction.wordpress.com

Henrik Obbekaer Rasmussen is a UK-educated Dane, now living between France and Switzerland. After a doctorate at Cambridge, Henrik spent a good quarter-century working as a mathematician within the financial sector, with stints in academia too, as a visiting fellow and then a lecturer at the University of Oxford. During a pandemic winter, he signed up for a creative-writing course at Cambridge, which led eventually to a Certificate and a couple of Diplomas. He is now working as a consultant in Zurich, while studying and writing in the evening. 'You buy books which you don't read. You write, then erase it all. What is the point?' his youngest son asks. As an émigré misfit, Henrik's main ambition is to be productive.

He dedicates *Café Mathematics* to the red-headed pianist S. B., who abhors the subject.

R L Shelley was once an architect building spaces, now he is a writer crafting worlds. His path has always been about creation, shaping clay as a potter, capturing fleeting moments as a photographer, burning things in a restaurant kitchen, and even directing the ambiance of a hotel. Now, he channels all of that into storytelling, approaching it with a designer's precision, an artist's eye, and just enough humour to keep things from feeling too serious.

In his latest work, he explores the notion of *hiraeth*, a deep, nostalgic longing for something intangible, something that perhaps never was. This emotion resonates in his narrative, as he creates stories of spaces to wander, of places filled with memory, mystery, and that bittersweet ache of things just out of reach. The story he writes is an invitation to explore a place familiar yet unknown, one page at a time.

www.rlshelley.com

Candy Smellie retired from the University of Cambridge in December 2020, but she had no intention of watching life pass her by. With a career in science communication behind her, she turned her attention to a long-standing passion: creative writing. Though social media marketing had offered glimpses of creativity, retirement finally gave her the freedom to fully embrace it. Armed with notebooks and a sense of purpose, she enrolled in the Institute of Continuing Education, completing both the Certificate and Diploma in Non-Fiction Creative Writing. But why stop there? The next challenge awaited. A Master's in Creative Fiction at Anglia Ruskin University, which she completed in October 2024.

Now, she's deeply immersed in the world of short stories,

contributing to multiple anthologies and discovering that this short form of storytelling, with its precision and power, is where her heart truly lies.

Beyond writing, Candy's life is just as vibrant. A lifelong choral singer, she continues to fill concert halls with music. She also spends cherished time with her grandsons, tends to her garden, and indulges her love of travel. To new adventures and new stories yet to be written.

www.candychorale.com

Caryn Solomon is a South African living in London. As a social psychologist, psychotherapist and lecturer, with a background in music, theatre and English literature, she spent forty years discovering the transformative impact of stories in both the telling and the hearing. Since retiring from university teaching and consulting internationally to many organisations in the fields of group dynamics, leadership and organisational change, she has, with five women from across the globe, co-written *Our Mothers Ourselves*, a celebration of their mothers, completed Certificate and Diploma courses in creative non-fiction at Cambridge University and now devotes herself full-time to writing creative non-fiction and short stories, which, she likes to believe, write her.

Fleeting Encounters, an anthology of short creative non-fiction pieces, co-written with five authors from diverse backgrounds, is soon to be published.

In *Kalahari Klip*, encountering herself anew in every place she has lived in and left behind, she discovers that what she is seeking is her childhood experience of innocence, warmth and belonging, rooted in Africa's light, landscape and weather.

Carey Somerville is a historian who has taught young children for over forty years, inspiring them with a love of creativity and of words. After completing creative non-fiction courses at the Cambridge Institute of Continuing Education, she is now revelling in the opportunity to write, drawing on her love of history, her experiences of teaching and of surviving a complex family.

Alison M. Templeton was moulded from the clay of Kent's Low Weald, then hurled up onto the chalk and flint of the North Downs. Most of her adult life she's shifted on sands and gravels, not her true substrate at all. She sometimes thinks she's an evolving ecological web herself.

A farming upbringing and degree in Rural Environment Studies at London University's Wye College, Alison worked in countryside management followed by partnership and community spheres alongside post-graduate studies at the University of the West of England. On retirement she returned to her first love, the natural world, and met her new best friend, writing.

Her Cambridge University writing qualification drew her into the collaboration for *Hiraeth*. Here her pen is spade, digging down into ideas, pored over with a hand lens, and examined through binoculars for form, colour and behaviour. In this way she investigates life's inner and outer intricacies and co-dependencies.

Fenna Williams lives in Wiesbaden, Germany, working as a freelance author and creative writing coach. Her previous role as an international tour guide offered her stories and insights in abundance. She gladly accepts that her memory is now a hiraeth treasure trove collected around the globe. The contents will inspire her writing for years to come.

Fenna studied literature and linguistics at FU Berlin and later creative fictional and non-fictional writing in Seattle and Cambridge. She has devoted herself to coaching colleagues of all genres and writing screenplays, short stories, crime novels and travel essays.

Under the pen name Auerbach & Auerbach, she composes the well-known crime series about house-sitter and translator Pippa Bolle, who is at home wherever a case takes her — just like her creator.

A versatile writer Fenna has won several prizes and grants. Her personal favourite, the 'Goldene Auguste', is a statuette awarded every three years to a person supporting the cause of crime-novels written in German by female authors world-wide.
www.Fenna-Williams.com

Klaudia Zotzmann-Koch lives in Vienna, Austria, about 800 kilometres away from where she grew up in a beautiful garden, which she misses dearly every day. She has always been a creative sort: singing in choirs, playing instruments, writing, and majoring in A-level art. She left her small German Vorharz-village to grow, becoming a freelance author, an IT-expert and a data privacy evangelist, working on topics that seep into her writing.

Klaudia studied English literature and philosophy at the university of Hannover, Germany, started (never finished) a PhD in philosophy at the University of Vienna, Austria and more recently, completed a diploma in creative non-fiction in Cambridge, UK.

She writes crime, sci-fi, historical fiction and non-fiction ranging from data privacy to now memoir writing. In *Hireath* she makes her first foray into this last genre.
www.zotzmann-koch.com

Also by The ICE Pack

Book Two

SAWUBONA — I See You

February 2026

'*Sawubona*', a simple yet profound Zulu greeting meaning 'I see you'. More than an acknowledgment, it is an honouring of another's existence. In Zulu culture, 'I' is never alone — we are all shaped by the whole; you are seen and welcomed by all that I am and all that came before me.

In this poignant collection sixteen authors reach beyond self, across countries, cultures and generations, bearing witness to those held close and those only glimpsed.

The authors invite you to enter a world where seeing is not merely looking but understanding, embracing.

Sawubona — we see you.

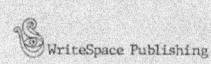WriteSpace Publishing

sawubona
/ˌsa(w)ʊˈbɔ(ː)na/
"I see you"

Edited by R. L. Shelley

Jo Cross, Jan Fuscoe, Chris Hayward, Mana Jay, Rowena Kilkelly, Pauline Hallam Mason, Barbara McMillan, Philippe Le Roux, Meike Schwagmann, R. L. Shelley, Candy Smellie, Caryn Solomon, Carey Somerville, Alison M. Templeton, Fenna Williams and Klaudia Zotzmann-Koch.

www.ingramcontent.com/pod-product-compliance
Ingram Content Group UK Ltd.
Pitfield, Milton Keynes, MK11 3LW, UK
UKHW041009130625
459610UK00003B/111